INCONSPICUOUS
CONSUMPTION

INCONSPICUOUS CONSUMPTION

An Obsessive Look

at the Stuff We Take for Granted,

from the Everyday

to the Obscure

PAUL LUKAS

Crown Trade Paperbacks
New York

For Henry and Mimi, who I'm sure would have enjoyed it

Copyright © 1997 by Paul Lukas

Published by Crown Trade Paperbacks, 201 East 50th Street, New York, New York 10022. Member of the Crown Publishing Group. Random House, Inc. New York, Toronto, London, Sydney, Auckland

http://www.randomhouse.com/

Crown Trade Paperbacks and colophon are trademarks of Crown Publishers, Inc.

Design by Blond on Pond

Photographs on pages 18, 19, 27, 70, 76, 98, 125, and 138 by Jasmine Redfern; all other photographs by Michael Galinsky.

Most of the reviews in this volume were first published in *New York Press*. A few first appeared in *NewCity, I.D.,* and *New York* magazine. All were subsequently reprinted in various issues of *Beer Frame: The Journal of Inconspicuous Consumption.*

Printed in the United States of America

Library of Congress Cataloging-in-Publication Data
Lukas, Paul.
    Inconspicuous consumption : an obsessive look at the stuff we take for granted, from the everyday to the obscure / Paul Lukas ; foreword by Steve Albini.
        p.   cm.
    1. Commercial products—Social aspects.   2. Consumer goods—Humor.
3. Material culture.   I. Title.
HM211.L85   1997
306.3—dc20   96-26550
                                                                                    CIP

ISBN: 0-517-88668-5

10 9 8 7 6 5 4 3 2 1

First Edition

CONTENTS

Acknowledgments

This project originally took shape in the fall of 1993, when I published the first issue of a fanzine called *Beer Frame: The Journal of Inconspicuous Consumption.* Like most 'zines, it was printed on an office copy machine when nobody was looking, collated and stapled by hand, and haphazardly distributed in an edition of a few hundred. The route from that living-room enterprise to this book has been a long and improbable one, and certainly could not have been traversed without the help of a great many people. I'd like to thank them now.

The first issue of *Beer Frame* quickly became the basis for my "Inconspicuous Consumption" column in *New York Press,* where Phyllis Orrick first saw the potential in the material, Russ Smith had the vision to run it as a regular column, and John Strausbaugh tastefully edited it every two weeks for over two years. Cindy Behrman, Ben Cohen, and Sam Sifton made invaluable contributions as well. In 1996 the column jumped over to *New York* magazine, where Mike Hirschorn was instrumental in acquiring it, Kurt Andersen was supportive of it, and Matt Weingarden has done a fine job of editing it. I'm grateful to all of them.

I tried to take inconspicuous consumption national during the column's early days, but found that while many magazine editors outside of New York were intrigued by what I was doing, few were willing to take a chance on it. The most notable exception was Brian Hieggelke of Chicago's *NewCity,* who reprinted some of my *Beer Frame* material and also gave me the idea (and the freedom) to write a book review column based exclusively on the book's physical properties, a great concept that I'm embarrassed not to have thought of first. Thanks, Brian.

Beer Frame has been lucky enough to attract some attention from a fair number of mainstream publications, as well as a few TV and radio shows—my thanks to any and all major-media journalists who took notice, especially Frank Flaherty at *The New York Times*, Becky Aikman at *Newsday*, Josh Glenn at *Utne Reader*, Victor Dorff at ABC-TV's *ABC World News Now*, Liane Hansen and Andrea Shea at National Public Radio's *Weekend Edition Sunday*, and Lisa Yapp at CNNfn's *Biz Buzz*, the latter of which eventually became the venue for a weekly televised version of my "Inconspicuous Consumption" column.

Of course, none of these media types would even have seen *Beer Frame* if not for the help I've had in producing it. I'm extremely fortunate to have had the support and assistance of a large number of friends and associates. Foremost among these is the charming and talented Jasmine Redfern, who has been *Beer Frame*'s official photographer right from the first issue, graciously allowing me to impose on her busy schedule and happily taking photo after photo of the assorted gadgets, oddball snack foods, and other consumer oddities that I routinely haul up to her apartment. Several of these photos have found their way into this book. Thanks, Jazzy—you're the best.

Other friends have given crucial assistance as well, whether by "attending" (i.e., working at) *Beer Frame* collating parties, suggesting or providing subjects for review, or just giving emotional support when I needed it. It's no exaggeration to say that this book would not exist in its current state if not for the efforts of each and every one of them. There are too many to list here, and I'm sure I'm forgetting quite a few, but those who deserve recognition include Barb Davies, Bonnie Schwartz, Gerry Mullany, Gretchen Colavito, Tim Karras, Ana Marie Cox, Joe Zizzo, Susan Singley, Tim Adams, Jay Anning, Bob Fillie, Scot Olive, Rich Kronenberg, John Gura, Brian Krall, Paula Ryan, Marian Appellof, Spike Vrusho, Jeff Hansen, Patrick O'Connor, Susan Mitchell, David G. Kramer, Will Hermes, Pagan Kennedy, Megan Montague Cash, Liz Clayton, Christine Wall, Irwin Lukas, Marilyn Lukas, Roy Lukas, Matt Weiland, Tom Frank, David Greenberger, Andrea Codrington,

Keira Alexandra, Sam Pratt, Mike LaVella, Brian Doherty, Barbara Powers, David Vodicka, John Darnielle, Marc Spiegler, John Marr, Ron Diorio, Daniel Radosh, Abby Bridge, Alex Jackson, Darcy Cosper, Skot Armstrong, Caroline Karlen, R. Seth Friedman, V. Vale, all of *Beer Frame*'s advertisers and distributors, and the scores of complete strangers who've sent me interesting products over the years (most accompanied by a note reading, "I saw this and thought of you"). My sincere thanks to one and all.

As for producing the book itself, I owe thanks to a great many people, particularly Mike Galinsky, who took most of the photos contained herein. Others who deserve mention include Steve Albini, who seemed as pleased and flattered to write the foreword as I was to have him do so; Sean Tejaratchi, who generously provided the dynamite illustrations for the chapter openers from his massive clip-art archive; and book designer Blond on Pond, production editor Jim Walsh, and production manager Judy Emery. A hearty handshake to all these folks.

Finally, a concept that seems fun and friendly to pursue in 'zine form can suddenly get very tedious once the business realities of the publishing world are added to the mix. Second helpings of thanks go to my agent, Kim Witherspoon, and her staff at Witherspoon Associates, and also to my editor at Crown, Wendy Hubbert, for making this project a pleasure from start to finish.

FOREWORD: AN APPRECIATION OF THINGS

I was born into a generation of ninnies. It has made me tired.

Almost to a man, we treat the world and its contents like a single immutable lump, unchanging and unappreciable. Things exist, and must be contended with, but their existence implies no perfection and their use is evidence only of their subjugation under our will. To remove oneself from this sphere requires transcendent insight, and such moments cannot be thrust upon us. We must make them.

In adolescence this mentality is forgivable. We are learning so much about ourselves and our influences as we mature that the things around us fade in importance. In order to distance myself from this embarrassment, I sometimes blame the thing-indifference of my youth on drinking and drugs, but in my heart I know I was preoccupied with sex and punk rock and didn't notice, much less appreciate, the greatness possible in the world of things.

Adulthood is when we wake up, if we do at all. Exposure to a wider variety of things, and having to rely on them, makes them become true and occasionally important. Some things work barely or not at all, while others work so perfectly that they make us take notice, not just of their efficiency or effectiveness but of their grace, the inventiveness they embody, and their unassuming beauty.

As this appreciation blossomed within me, it became obvious that the greatness of things is everywhere, requiring only the patience and temperament to notice. Utility, beauty, art, permanence, and craftsmanship sometimes come bundled in one thing, and that thing is then Great and Perfect. Anything from a bottle of pop or a cigarette lighter to a giant machine that makes other things can be both Great and Perfect, and appreciating them as they crop up in our lives is the essence of Paul Lukas's doctrine of inconspicuous consumption.

As I became aware of things myself, I realized there were others who were aware of things. Endeavoring to find them, my gaze instinctively moved to the mantelpiece, bookshelf, cabinet, or closet when I entered a new place. Were they bedecked with brilliant things? What art or science lives here? Are these people Aware? Conversation always erupted among the Aware, as they demonstrated and reveled in the genius of their prizes. Evenings never lasted long enough—there always seemed to be one more trophy to show, one more story of discovery, one more poem of appreciation to recite before we returned to the company of the ninnies.

Inconspicuous consumption's passive practice has a relaxing and subtle charm as well. We may linger while observing or handling a thing slightly longer than absolutely necessary to make use of it, and idle time may be enriched by seeing whether things have worth beyond their intended utility. Appreciation of things can also be expanded beyond the physical. There is room on the stage of appreciation, beside the matchboxes and shoe trees of greatness, for all the services, lectures, lessons, and indefinable experiences that ultimately reveal themselves to be Great and Perfect.

Which things do we appreciate? Things that, through perfection in design, concept, and execution, are beautiful, do their job immaculately well, and continue to do so forever. They exist and we can know them. Awareness is all.

STEVE ALBINI

Introduction: What Is Inconspicuous Consumption?

What is inconspicuous consumption?

People are always asking me that, so you'd think I'd have figured out an answer by now. As it happens, however, the concept of inconspicuous consumption is frustratingly difficult to pin down — it seems to actively resist my efforts to define it. But we have to begin somewhere, so let's start with this: *Inconspicuous consumption is about paying attention to the details of consumer culture. It's about noticing certain aspects of products and services we might otherwise overlook, things that are either so obscure that we never see them or so ubiquitous that we've essentially stopped seeing them.*

This sounds simple enough at first glance, but in fact it implies a pretty broad range of purview. I like to think of my potential subject area as, simply, Everything. But which subset of Everything is worth writing about? My preferences tend to run toward light-industrial gadgets, bizarre foodstuffs, products that serve as solutions to problems I hadn't even considered, inadvertently ironic marketing pitches, and just about anything in an interesting package. But that's just a starting point. Look around and you'll see there's a bonanza of thought-provoking stuff out there — some of it unusual, much of it exceedingly ordinary, but all worthy of close inspection.

This is truer than ever in today's bloated information market. Every new magazine or cable TV channel — or Web site, for that matter — is another opportunity for advertisers to wedge their collective foot into the door of our consciousness, presenting more and more products for our consideration. Some people find this disgusting, others revel in it, but personally I'm not here to bury consumerism *or* to praise it. Like a lot of smart people who grew up watching television, I approach the overall consumer experience with a bit of ambivalence —

call it measured enthusiasm mixed with a healthy cynicism. The main thing I try to remember is that the consumer landscape presents interesting opportunities for learning things on both a personal and cultural level, including new answers to questions I'd thought had long been settled and the transformation of the implicit into the explicit. For me, a good product is one that makes me think, one that teaches me something. Sometimes it gets me thinking about the product itself, sometimes about some greater aspect of consumerism, and sometimes just about me.

Ah yes — me. Ultimately, all of the preceding analysis is subordinate to the following maxim: *Inconspicuous consumption is whatever I say it is.* Consumerism, in spite of advertisers' and marketers' relentless attempts to render it generic, remains an intensely personal experience, with each of us intersecting the consumer plane in our own highly individualized manner. As a result, this book's content is primarily a function of whichever products have pushed my personal buttons; your mileage may vary. And much as I hate to invoke the old Supreme Court cop-out, I'm afraid the best answer to the question posed at the top of this essay is this: I may not be able to define inconspicuous consumption, but *I know it when I see it.*

Here's where I've seen it recently.

ONE

GADGETS

Given that human beings are made of flesh and blood, it's funny how we're fascinated by machines built of metal, circuits, and wire. Gadgets hold an intuitive appeal for most of us, especially if they feature an assortment of sprockets, gears, sliding pieces, and switches. Why? Because even the most cynical adult is still just a big, overgrown kid, and kids never outgrow the need for toys. These gadgets offer a wide range of specialized practical utility, to be sure. But they also offer something else: a chance to play.

Here we have the quintessential example of inconspicuous consumption. The Brannock Device, invented in 1926 by one Charles F. Brannock, is that gizmo they use to measure your shoe size. Given this rather workaday function, it is a product of remarkable design values: chrome and black metal, a splendidly balanced asymmetry (much like, surprise, the human foot itself), two parts that pleasingly slide back and forth, graduated calibration markings all over the place —really a near-perfect combination of the industrial and the aesthetic. Yes, I have one of my very own, and while I don't exactly put it under my pillow at night, I do like to pick it up periodically, hold it, play with it—it's a very *tactile* product.

Why is the Brannock Device so prototypically inconspicuous? Consider: everyone has come into contact with it, but nobody knows what it's called. I find that if you describe the Brannock Device to anyone —*anyone*— they'll most likely say, "Oh yeah, thing's really cool—I never thought about it before." Precisely. Moreover, most of us first encounter the Brannock Device during childhood, which means our Brannock memories tend to be simultaneously primal and nostalgic—a potent combination.

Charles Brannock died in 1992 at the age of 89. He was a lifelong bachelor, married only to his invention. It's worth noting, however, that while he may have invented a dandy device, his company has displayed a rather niggardly attitude toward sharing it with the likes of you and me. Unless you're a shoe store or a shoe-supply distributor, they won't even talk about selling you a Brannock Device, no matter how much cash you offer (or how complimentary a product review you promise to write). So find yourself a shoe store that'll order you one (I had to go to several before finding a willing accomplice), and while you're there, pick up a $2 can of Kiwi shoe polish, which features a fine package design for you to admire while you're waiting for your Brannock Device to arrive.

THE
BRANNOCK DEVICE
COMPANY,
INC.

THE AMERICAN SONG WHISTLE

anna get your hands on a well-designed, well-made, inexpensive toy? Wanna pretend you know how to play a musical instrument? Wanna make a sound so weird that nobody around you will know whether to be annoyed or amused? Then run down to your local music store, throw down a $20 bill on the counter, and ask for a slide whistle. You'll get back seven or eight bucks and one of the coolest products ever invented.

Even in strictly aesthetic terms, the slide whistle (or the American Song Whistle, as it is officially known) shows all the signs of delivering a superior consumer experience. With its all-chrome construction, pleasing weight (substantial, but not so heavy that it's a chore to lift), and a sliding piece with a handle designed at a screwball angle, it's obviously an instrument but just as obviously a gadget, and that's my kind of product.

Once you stop admiring the slide whistle long enough to pick it up, put the appropriate end to your lips, grab the slide handle, and blow. When you stop giggling, try it again. You'll soon find that you can duplicate the entire range of sound effects used to punctuate Wile E. Coyote's unfortunate plunges off of steep cliffs in Roadrunner cartoons. You'll also be able to reproduce any melody in no time flat, but the transition from note to note will have a very slippery, slurred quality, sort of like the way Bill Murray used to sing in his lounge-act skits on *Saturday Night Live.* The overall sound is incredibly synthetic, which makes this product's simplicity all the more impressive.

AMERICAN
PLATING &
MANUFACTURING
CO.

The slide whistle is a guaranteed hit with kids, but its sound can grate on the nerves after a while — probably sooner on yours than on the average eight-year-old's — so I wouldn't recommend just handing one over to your nephew.

"MR. BLINKER" CLIP-ON SIGNAL LIGHTS

B eing an inconspicuous consumer can have its drawbacks, especially when you're so damn inconspicuous that your friendly neighborhood bartender doesn't even see that you've finished your drink and would very much like another. It's happened to all of us at one time or another: you rattle your empty glass along the bar, but he's busy yakking with another customer; you slide over a buck or two as an early tip, but he doesn't notice; you feel rejected, ignored, overlooked, and, let's not forget, thirsty.

It was with this problem in mind that some early-1960s merchandising whiz came up with Mr. Blinker, a four-inch-long penlight with a clip-on attachment. Can't get Joe Bartender's attention? Don't fret—just clip Mr. Blinker onto the lip of your glass. The clip acts as a switch, activating the small bulb inside, which shines steadily for 15 to 30 seconds and then starts blinking. Let's see Joe try to ignore *that*.

Of course, this approach may not appeal to everyone. When I showed Mr. Blinker to my own friendly neighborhood bartender, Patrick O'Connor—a man who *never* fails to attend to a glass in need—he was not impressed. "It's an insult to the profession of bartending," he sniffed, which probably goes a long way toward explaining why Mr. Blinker never caught on. Too bad. I find the thought of a dozen tavern patrons scattered down the length of a bar, each with a Mr. Blinker clipped onto his glass, enormously appealing.

Mr. Blinker comes two to a box —a very nice box, I might add— and usually arrives with a pair of long-dead but beautifully designed vintage AA batteries from 30-odd years ago (you have to supply fresh ones). Unfortunately, Mr. B's

19

packaging doesn't list a manufacturer or distributor. This is a shame, as I'd hoped to contact the company and chat with someone about the whole Mr. Blinker saga (if ever there was a product that *had* to have begun as a few scribblings on a cocktail napkin, this is it).

Mr. Blinker is no longer in production, sadly. I got my box for $1.75 from American Science & Surplus, a mail-order firm that puts out an amusing catalog of small, interesting surplus objects, most of them much more light-industrial and less kitschy than Mr. Blinker. They describe Mr. B as "Dumb Idea #372," which is the sort of praising with faint damnation that barely hints at this product's brilliant entertainment value.

SMOKER'S ROBOT

O ne of the most amusing little gadgets I've encountered is the Smoker's Robot, which in spite of its name does *not* involve a little android who smokes with or for you. This robot is much simpler. It's a chrome-plated ashtray with a metal cigarette holder projecting upward about 1.25 inches from the ashtray's base at roughly a 75-degree angle. Sticking out from the side of the ashtray is a thin, flexible plastic tube nearly a yard long, which is connected to the cigarette holder at a concealed point within the base and terminates in a hard plastic mouthpiece.

You've no doubt figured out the rest already. You light up a cigarette, stick it in the holder, suck on the mouthpiece at the end of the tube, and, well, there you are—you're smoking. Because the holder is angled, the cigarette extends right over the ashtray and deposits its ashes therein. Meanwhile, you have both hands free for other things. If so inclined, you can even run laps in a three-foot radius around the Robot.

If this doesn't sound like fun, trust me — it is. There's nothing like a toy or a gadget to turn any simple task, even smoking, into an enjoyable game, and I'm fairly certain that even the most jaded play instinct will be aroused by the Smoker's Robot. It's also entertaining to see the ash end of the disembodied cigarette glow brighter when you take a drag on the mouthpiece. In spite of the obvious conduit provided by the tube, the cig almost appears to be smoking itself.

The Smoker's Robot's makers tout it as the ideal product for smoking "where dozing may occur," although they're careful not to actually suggest smoking in bed. Fine, I'll suggest it myself. The thought of a Smoker's Robot on everyone's night table — maybe "His" and "Hers" versions for couples — sounds pretty nifty to me. At the very least, it could revolutionize the postcoital cigarette. As the Robot's box points out, this product also makes "a thoughtful gift for the convalescent, and 'Lazybones' will find it thrilling too."

The Smoker's Robot was invented in the 1950s by Jonathan Law, a gift wholesaler. After Law's death, his company was purchased in 1981 by one of his longtime employees, Elaine Swett. She told me that today's typical Robot customer is bound to either a bed or a wheelchair, with most sales coming through veterans' hospitals and nursing homes.

As Swett sees it, she's not exactly operating in a growth market. "Sales have dropped considerably," she reported, although she declined to discuss precise figures. Swett, who now constitutes 100 percent of the Jonathan Law workforce, attributes the slowdown to the recent proliferation of anti-smoking regulations and the corresponding smoke-free mood in the land.

It seems to me that this state of affairs presents an interesting opportunity for both Swett and the beleaguered tobacco industry. Swett needs to break into new markets and lower the average age of her demographic; the cigarette manufacturers, who long ago ran out of ways to make smoking look sexy, glamorous, or macho, need a gimmick to make smoking look simply *fun*. I hereby suggest some sort of cross-promotional licensing deal, and I won't even demand too big a cut of the proceeds.

DIAL-A-PICK TOOTHPICK DISPENSER, MODEL S-11

I've never had much use for religion, but that all changed one spring day in Austin when my pal Ana and I were having breakfast at the G.M. Steakhouse, one of the greasiest greasy-spoon diners I've ever had the pleasure of visiting. I'd finished my French toast, Ana had polished off her eggs, and I was up at the register waiting to pay the bill, when I suddenly found God.

God appeared to me in the form of a stainless-steel gizmo sitting next to the cash register. It was slightly smaller than a napkin dispenser, with a ridged knob protruding from one side and a tiny rack extending outward from the base of the front panel. I reached out, turned the knob, and was rewarded with the pleasing sight of a solitary toothpick being deposited onto the rack. It rocked back and forth for an instant and then came to rest, ready for use. I was entranced.

It had all happened so quickly, I hadn't properly taken note of the mechanics involved. So I removed the first toothpick and tried again, this time turning the knob more slowly and taking care to observe the details of what transpired.

First of all, the bulk of the gadget was obviously filled with toothpicks. And the knob, I now saw, was connected to a counterweighted cylinder sitting horizontally inside the lower portion of the dispenser. When I turned the knob, I was also turning the cylinder, which, as I also noted, was not perfectly cylindrical after all—a narrow notch had been carved down its length, just wide enough to house a toothpick. The cylinder, thanks to its unbalanced weight, automatically returned to its predispensing position once I let go of the knob, at which point a fresh toothpick loaded into the notch. When the knob and cylinder were turned again, the toothpick rode down in the notch until it fell, neatly and cleanly, into the rack.

Admit it: As gods go, this one's pretty cool.

Understanding how the thing worked heightened its appeal—it was all so smooth, so functional, a beautiful example of industrial design. I stood there, a smile on my face, turning the knob again and again. Fortunately, just as my newfound religious fervor began to border on fanaticism, Ana brought me back to reality with a gentle nudge, a nod toward the mountain of toothpicks I'd dispensed, and a softly worded inquiry: "Uh, Paul . . . What were you planning to do with all of those?"

Okay, so I got a bit carried away. After regaining my bearings, I took a quick peek at the dispenser's back panel and learned that the object of my obsession was a Dial-a-Pick, model S-11—an odd guise for God to assume, admittedly, but then the Lord has always moved among us in truly humble fashion.

Upon returning home to

New York a few days later, I gave a call to Dial-a-Pick Central and spoke with company manager and sole employee/apostle Sidney Kempler. He explained that the Dial-a-Pick is the only product the firm sells and that the S-11, immaculately conceived in the 1940s by a now-deceased merchant marine sailor named Irving Mayer, is the only model available. As for spreading the gospel, Kempler said he moves about 10,000 Dial-a-Picks per year — not a sufficient number to compete with, say, Pat Robertson, it's true, but enough to ensure that the Church of Dial-a-Pick will continue to maintain a presence, however modest, throughout the land.

GALIL AUTOMATIC TRAFFIC RECORDER

I was getting into my car one day when I noticed one of those traffic box gizmos on the sidewalk. You've probably seen them — the boxes have a plain metal exterior and are usually chained to something solid, like a lamppost. A rubber tube typically protrudes from the box and out into the street, where it's often duct-taped onto the pavement, presumably to measure traffic patterns.

I'd seen the boxes before but hadn't really *noticed* them, if you know what I mean — they were sufficiently inconspicuous to fly beneath my radar. On this day, however, I took a closer look at the box, found a sticker indicating that it belonged to a Staten Island firm called American Traffic Information, and made a mental note to find out more.

The next morning I called ATI and chatted with project manager Kurt Kratchman, who explained that the boxes are called automatic traffic recorders. By digitizing the data impressions made by cars going over the rubber tube, the recorders can measure the volume and speed of traffic on a given stretch of road, as well as which types of vehicles are passing by, from bicycles to 18-wheelers. The information is stored in the recorder's memory and eventually downloaded to a computer. A pretty sophisticated gadget, especially considering the plain-Jane box that houses it. Personally, I like this low-key approach — with all the ridiculous products clamoring for our attention, it's nice to find one that's so . . . modest.

ATI offers traffic-monitoring and data-collection services to government planning agencies, businesses considering whether to operate near this or that site, and so on. From the early eighties through the mid-nineties they used other firms' recorder boxes, but when I spoke to Kratchman, they were just getting ready to begin manufacturing their own. The box I encountered, called the Galil, runs on common AA batteries; it's airtight and watertight, which makes it largely immune to the vagaries of weather (although not to vandals, snowplows, paving crews, or drunk drivers). Once it's mass-produced, ATI plans to sell it for about $500.

Kratchman said the concept of recording traffic data began around the 1930s, when WPA-financed roadway projects began proliferating around the country. At the time, this meant standing by the side of the road with a pen and a clipboard, counting what went by. Automatic recorders were pioneered by the British, who used them for military purposes during World War II. They entered civilian use during the fifties in the United States, when the development of America's burgeoning highway system moved into high gear. Today, ATI is expecting big business from the third world, where highway development is ripe to explode. Which just goes to show that American ingenuity can even deploy something as seemingly mundane as traffic engineering to exploit the little guy.

AMERICAN TRAFFIC INFORMATION, INC.

TWO

Some things are inconspicuous because they're too obscure to be seen. At the other end of the spectrum, however, are products that hide in plain sight, so to speak — products we see almost every day but whose subtler aspects have long since fallen from our collective field of vision, products we see so often that we've essentially *stopped* seeing them. What follows is an assortment of items that I've found deserving of a closer look.

VICTOR MOUSE TRAP

Build a better one of these, as the saying goes, and the world will beat a path to your door. But trust me, there are easier ways to meet women than that. Besides, who needs a better one when this model here is perfectly adequate? Look at all these fine features: high-quality spring mechanism, cool logo stamped into the wood, pleasingly organic combination of wood and wire (this in stark contrast to the Pic Corporation's Katch 'Em! trap, which has a bright yellow plastic bait tray, eckh!). And did you ever devote a few moments to studying how these things actually operate? The whole mechanism is incredibly simple, and rather ingeniously so. Plus, at two for $1.39, you get a fair amount of ruthlessly efficient bang for the buck.

For those who want more, try Woodstream's Victor Rat Trap, an industrial-strength doozy that's essentially a double-your-pleasure version of the above. Set it up, leave it out on the hallway table, and then place your rent check over it; soon they'll be calling your landlord "Lefty." As for whether any of this stuff actually works on rodents, I really have no idea, and I have no intention of finding out — I *like* mice.

WOODSTREAM CORPORATION

POLE-MOUNTED MAILBOX • • • • • • • • • • • • • • • • •

W hen I say "mailbox," I'm not talking about the place at your home where your mail is delivered. Nor am I referring to the four-legged structure that can be found on every third or fourth street corner. I'm talking about its diminutive cousin, the pole-mounted letterbox that can still be found occasionally among the seven square acres of America that are officially designated as "the heartland."

I don't actually own one of these boxes yet, and I haven't yet discovered how to obtain one without employing a hacksaw, but it's definitely high on my list. The merits of this product should be apparent to anybody who's ever used one: solid cast-iron construction, timeless color palette, pleasing miniaturization of a familiar form, the trusty *cr-r-ree-eea-kk!* of the heavily counterweighted door to the letter slot—you get the idea. Best of all, if you look closely

UNITED
STATES POSTAL
SERVICE

you'll notice that all such mailboxes are mounted on an identical official, U.S.P.S.-specified pole: a pebble-and-concrete affair that tapers from its base to a point at the top, sort of like a tiny Washington Monument —a living example of the sort of industrial design standardization that has utterly failed to make this country what it is today.

MAIL CHUTE

I f the pole-mounted mailbox represents the micro-postal experience, then the mail chute clearly offers the macropostal alternative. Mail chutes may not be as cool as pneumatic tubes, but they still add some fun to even the dreariest office high-rise. You know the routine: drop your letter in the slot, watch for an instant as it disappears down the chute, and then listen in vain for audible evidence of its arrival in the box in the building lobby.

The key to the interactive consumer experience here is that the chute is *transparent,* a design decision for which we should all be grateful. They could've made the whole chute out of steel or aluminum or whatever, and that would've taken the fun out of the game. You'd drop your letter in the slot and that would be the last you'd see of it, just like when using a normal letterbox, big deal. But because the chute is transparent, you get those few instants of seeing your letter beginning its gravity-driven trip down into the belly of the building.

For me, those critical moments test and ultimately reinforce the magic of the postal system. Being able to *see* the envelope beginning its 39-floor descent highlights the letter's mortality. It looks vulnerable, innocent, a small fish in a huge postal pond. Did it somehow turn sideways and get wedged against the wall around the 17th floor? Did someone try to shove a small package in the chute, leading to a huge pile-up of letters between floors 11 and 12? Despite these and other paranoias, I ultimately have enough faith in the chute to keep going back for more.

Another nice thing about the transparent chute, of course, is that you can watch other letters flying by from higher floors. If my father had worked in a high-rise office

UNITED STATES POSTAL SERVICE

building with a mail chute, and if he had brought me to work one morning when I was seven years old so that I could see what he did all day long, I'm sure I would've spent the entire day staring at the chute, watching the mail go by. As it happens, my father owned a ground-floor shop in a two-story building, so I never had this experience, which may explain why I felt compelled to stare at the chute at my first high-rise job when I was 26.

WOOLBLEND MARK

The familiar Woolmark (left) and the more inconspicuous Woolblend mark.

 e're all familiar with the Woolmark, that vaguely gyroscopic-looking symbol that appears on pure wool apparel, upholstery, and carpeting. Designed in the mid-1960s for the International Wool Secretariat by the Italian designer Francesco Sarolgia, it has since become a ubiquitous presence in our lives.

What you may not know, however, is that in 1972 the IWS introduced a second, more inconspicuous symbol, the Woolblend mark. It looks like a cheap, less satisfying version of the Woolmark, sort of the way wool blends look and feel like cheap, less satisfying versions of wool. I discovered the Woolblend mark while looking over some promotional materials that had been loaned to me by a friend in the textile field. My interest aroused, I called the Wool Bureau (the United States branch of the IWS), where the very helpful Pat Eells explained that the Woolblend mark is bestowed upon apparel and upholstery with a wool content of at least 60 percent; for carpeting, the threshold is 80 percent. Since wool blends are nothing to brag about in the fashion world, where any synthetic-fiber content tends to be frowned upon, most clothing manufacturers opt not to use the Woolblend mark at all, accounting for its low visibility.

Pat went on to explain that fabrics bearing either of the two symbols must meet assorted IWS-mandated standards of strength, durability, colorfastness, cleanability, and so on. In an effort to see that these quality-control standards are upheld, the IWS administers a rigorous battery of textile torture tests at its labs in Ilkley, England. Pat wasn't sure whether the stain-resistance evaluations entail testing the fabrics with cat hair balls, but personal experience leads me to doubt it.

Since I already had Pat on the phone, I decided to quiz her about the promo literature's interesting claim that the Woolmark is "the world's most widely recognized symbol of quality." When I asked her on what basis this statement was made, she nonchalantly replied, "Braggadocio." When pressed, she explained, "I'm pretty sure that it is [the most widely recognized], but I can't prove it. We did surveys once, but I'm not sure how up-to-date they are." With a press liaison like Pat, the Wool Bureau may want to develop a new symbol soon — something along the lines of a person chatting with a writer, with one of those red circle-slashes going through it.

THE
WOOL BUREAU,
INC.

ALPO GOURMET DINNER DRY CAT FOOD, 18-OUNCE BOX

When package designers aren't busy dreaming up new ways for us to feel like we're moving up a notch on the cultural totem pole (as if plunking down $3.99 for some classy-looking stoned-wheat crackers will really make us genteel and erudite), their favorite trick is suggesting, through a simple packaging alteration, that a product has been overhauled and improved. When we see one of those flashy, exploding announcements that say, "Great New Flavor!" —in the biz, this is known as a "burst"—we all know it isn't the promise of the new flavor that we're responding to. It's the change in the packaging, in the form of the announcement itself, that excites us.

ALPO PETFOODS, INC.

This train of thought caught up with me recently in my grocer's cat food aisle. As I surveyed the usual assortment of dry foods and tried to decide which brand Barbarella might be hankering for, something about the familiar Alpo box caught my eye. In the upper-right corner was a burst: "New Package Design!" And that was it—no fine-print details, no explanation on the side panel. Moreover, aside from the burst itself, I couldn't figure out *anything* different about the packaging—it looked like the same product I'd been buying for months. (Only several days later did I realize they'd made a marginal change in the way the box is opened.)

It seems to me that Alpo has come up with the first postmodern burst. The self-referential genius in having a package design crow about itself essentially acknowledges that the packaging was all we (or they) ever cared about in the first place. This approach may be cynical, but it's also honest—I'd nonetheless like to suggest that all captains of industry take note and follow suit.

ETCH-A-SKETCH MAGIC SCREEN

W ith this product now showing up in trendy design stores, it's barely worth stating the increasingly obvious, so I'll get right to the point: every home should have one of these.

The last time you saw an Etch-A-Sketch was probably when you were a bratty six-year-old throwing it at your kid brother's head, so it's definitely time for a new one. Its basic pleasures are the same as always — a good way to satisfy the creative urge, work off tension, etc. — but you might be surprised at some of its potential adult-oriented applications. To wit, you can (1) create an abstract Etch-A-Sketch doodle, photograph it, and send it to the National Endowment for the Arts, along with a request for a $20,000 grant "to further my artistic development"; (2) kidnap some rich sap, dump him in a hole for safekeeping, and use your Etch-A-Sketch to create a new standard in untraceable ransom notes (don't forget to wear gloves); (3) when your sweetie comes home at

two in the morning smelling like a liquor store and claims to have been working late at the office, challenge him to write his name with the Etch-A-Sketch; and (4) when he fails, throw it at his head. See how life works in cycles?

Plus, for only $4, you can join the Official Etch-A-Sketch Club, entitling you to an Official Etch-A-Sketch Club membership card, an Official Etch-A-Sketch Club sew-on patch, and a subscription to the Official Etch-A-Sketch newsletter, which is packed with exciting Etch-A-Sketch news, including the names and addresses of Etch-A-Sketch pen pals! Yowie-kazowie.

BAND-AID ADHESIVE BANDAGES

When it comes to ubiquitous products, a change in packaging is generally more interesting to me than an alteration in the item itself. Unfortunately, most packaging changes these days are for the worse — cost-cutting maneuvers that usually sacrifice utility and interactive consumer pleasure in favor of graphic hype and the short-term bottom line.

But what is the proper response to a packaging change that undeniably improves the product, but at the expense of aesthetic satisfaction? This is the question that's been running through my mind ever since my friend Marian pointed out that Band-Aids no longer come packaged with that little red tear string. Instead, in order to open an individual Band-Aid, you just peel apart the flared tips at the end of its wrapper.

There's no getting around it, the peel-down wrap is easier to use than the tear string, which always seemed to get stuck or jammed. But the loss in product charm is palpable — after all, what's a Band-Aid without the little red string? It's like a Bic ballpoint pen without the little hole in the center of the tube, or a bottle of aspirin without the wad of cotton. As Marian put it, "Even though I could never get the strings to work when I was bleeding all over the place, I still thought they were . . . well, the way Band-Aids were supposed to be. Next they'll be getting rid of the metal cans."

Actually, they've already done that, at least with some varieties. A quick trip to my local drugstore revealed that in the half-dozen or so years since I last purchased Band-Aids (doesn't everyone have an ancient can of them in the medicine cabinet?), the product line has grown by proverbial leaps and bounds, with several styles now coming in a *cardboard* box. Packaging aside, the sheer array of current Band-

Aid offerings borders on the ridiculous, taking up yards of valuable shelf space that would be better devoted to such underrated products as nail clippers or styptic pencils. You could bleed to death while contemplating which Band-Aids to purchase: Plastic Strips, Sheer Strips, Sport Strips ("For active people"), Medicated ("Germ-fighting protection"), Clear (" 'Invisible' protection," which'll really trick those nasty germs), Flexible Fabric ("Contoured protection"), Hot Colors ("Fun protection"), Sesame Street (ditto), and Glow in the Dark ("Safe, fun protection, all in one," which I gather is code for, "Don't worry, parents—they're not radioactive").

Reeling from Band-Aid overload, I called the Johnson & Johnson consumer-response line, where a well-trained representative informed me that the tear string had been discontinued in 1993 in order to make the product easier-opening, ending a 53-year reign of packaging dominance. And while Marian and I may be torn over the pros and cons of this move, Johnson & Johnson maintains that no such ambivalence exists in the larger consumer marketplace. "People were surprised but glad," reported my J&J contact, who said she'd received many calls on the matter. "They found the string quite frustrating to use at times, especially when they already had a cut." But surely *someone* must have complained about the loss of the string, right? Not really, I was told. Such is the self-justifying psyche of the corporate monolith.

As for the metal cans (or "tins," as my J&J rep anachronistically and inaccurately termed them), I was informed that they are now reserved for new product lines, special promotions, and low-quantity packs. But there are no plans to discontinue them entirely, which is good news for anyone who finds immense satisfaction, as I do, in the sound and the feel of the timeless, metallic "click!" that reverberates when the lid to the can is snapped shut.

JOHNSON
& JOHNSON
CONSUMER
PRODUCTS, INC.

OFFICE CHAIR

My life took an unexpected turn for the better when I was 22, when the draconian employer for whom I then toiled moved me to a new workstation, complete with a new chair. As chairs go, this one didn't seem very special—your basic four legs, cheesy upholstery, no arm-rests, no reclining action or anything fancy like that. The backrest, in fact, seemed a bit skimpier than most, falling about a foot shy of the thronelike proportions of my previous work seat. Then one day I took a few moments to stretch out and lean back in the chair.

Cr-rr-ra-aa-aa-cc-ck-kk! The short backrest lodged in just the right spot in my spine, setting off a chain reaction of back-cracking that sounded like a cross between a machine gun and a string of firecrackers. I'd already been an obses-sive knuckle-cracker for years, and therefore knew that joint-cracking always follows something of a tension/release model, but back-cracking, as I soon learned, is positively orgastic. The process of twisting my spine inside out was so intensely pleasurable that I'd sort of black out for an instant; when I surfaced a moment later, I'd find myself in a state of hazy bliss, my body suddenly in a loosey-goosey condition I can only describe as gelatinous. I never had the urge for a cigarette, but I was definitely in no condition to operate heavy machinery. Within a minute or two I'd be ready to resume the daily grind, but with a markedly happier feeling resonating through my body.

Unfortunately, this symbiotic relationship with the chair came to an end several months later, when I changed jobs. Worse still, I foolishly neglected to write down the chair's manufacturer and model, assuming I'd be

STYLEX,
INC.

able to locate substitute seating with little difficulty. As things turned out, I never encountered another chair exactly like that one, despite five years of periodic trips to office-furniture outlets. Back-cracking attempts on other models proved fruitless. The pressure in my spine approached critical mass.

Then, finally, I moved to a new office with a new chair. The moment I saw it, I *knew*. It had different upholstery, and had armrests, but it wasn't just any chair—it was *that* chair. I quietly sat down, leaned back, and felt the cathartic rush of a half-decade's worth of tension exploding out of my body. While my productivity was not at its highest for the rest of that day—I was too busy staring into space with a big grin on my face—I can honestly say that a daily diet of subsequent back-cracking has gone a long way toward keeping me healthy and happy while tethered to my desk for eight hours a day. No joke, people—screw the chiropractor and just get yourself a good chair.

BETTER HOUSEWARE SELF-CLEANING GARLIC PRESS

I don't know what draws such women to me, or me to them, but none of my last four girlfriends has owned a garlic press. Two of them had never had occasion to use a garlic press, and one, whose mother's culinary skills tend toward the frozen and processed, had never even *heard* of a garlic press.

All of which strikes me as a tremendous drag, because garlic presses, when properly designed, are beautifully utilitarian objects. While I may be biased, I nonetheless maintain that the best garlic press I've ever encountered resides on a pegboard in my mother's suburban kitchen, a proud veteran of over four decades' worth of garlic wars. Attractively contoured, sturdily constructed, utterly functional, and by now splendidly burnished, it's everything a cherished kitchen implement should be.

BETTER
HOUSEWARE
CORP.

Unfortunately, I've never been able to locate another garlic press just like my mom's, so I gather it's no longer in production. My attempts to come up with a suitable substitute have been rather unfulfilling: there was the one whose garlic hopper was too small; the one whose cheapo handle snapped in two when confronted with an oversized garlic clove (served me right for buying a plastic-handled press); the one that was inexplicably and infuriatingly designed with two little nubs, one on each handle, that actually *prevented* the press from completely crushing the cloves in the hopper; the one that stank endlessly of garlic after the first use, no matter how much I washed it — don't even get me started, it's all too depressing.

Instead, let's just proceed directly to the Better Houseware garlic press, a nice little stainless job I picked up at a hardware store a few years ago for all of five bucks. Like so many successful examples of functional industrial design, this one is beautiful in its simplicity: pleasingly solid, two no-frills handles, an inside-out self-cleaning capability, no yuppie design flourishes or colored-plastic accented details. Just the facts, ma'am. The generous hopper easily accommodates two medium-sized cloves at a time, and the two handles fit satisfyingly into my palm when I squeeze them together. When the press descends into the hopper, those cloves don't stand a chance. Of all the items in my possession, I can't think of another that fulfills its intended role so simply, thoroughly, and efficiently.

KOTEX DISCREET SUPER ABSORBENCY TAMPONS, 20-COUNT BOX

O ne of the nice things about obsessing over the world of consumer culture is the way I keep finding intellectual stimulation, or at least entertainment value, in products and services I really have no business encountering in the first place. Simple biology, for example, may have rendered me ill-equipped to utilize Kotex Discreet tampons, at least in the usual way (there are other ways, as we'll see in a minute), but that doesn't mean I can't be fascinated by them all the same.

The initial gimmick behind Kotex Discreet lies in the product's no-frills method of engagement. These tampons are applicator-free, which means the actual product is just two inches long, a mere jellybean compared to the cigar-like proportions of most applicator-inclusive tampon assemblages. While this design scheme may not be new (o.b. tampons have been offering this same option for years), I think Kotex's marketing angle might be.

The Discreet name, of course, implies discretion, and this is where things get interesting. The product's diminutive size is a de facto suggestion of prudence, and a more explicit boast along these same lines can be found on the back of the Kotex Discreet box: "Bright and colorful wrap, so only you know it's a Discreet tampon." This claim, despite its appealingly literal embodiment of inconspicuous consumption, is rather puzzling. I mean, a tampon is *inherently* inconspicuous —who besides the user would see the damn thing anyway? Tampons are usually kept out of sight, which means all the fuss about the wrapper is really a wash, especially in the case of a product that can fit in your pants pocket. And besides, the real issue here is private use versus public use: on the one hand, once you and your tampon retreat to the isolation of a bathroom stall, all notions of packaging discretion are rendered moot anyway; on the other, if you're suddenly gripped by the urge to deploy a Kotex Discreet while riding the crosstown bus, I think everyone's gonna know what you're up to, no matter how deceptive the wrapper might be.

As for the wrapper itself, well, they're right — it *is* bright and colorful. Downright festive, in fact. While the primary intent of the bouncy color palette and bows-and-ribbons design may be, as claimed, diversionary, I see other possibilities. The wrappers' jaunty visuals, combined with the tampons' smallish size, create the inescapable suggestion of candy. So much so, in fact, that I went out and bought a box of Kotex Discreet, dumped the lot of them into a bowl, and displayed the bowl on my coffee table, where it garners interesting reactions from my houseguests. And I also have something unique to give to the kids on Halloween.

KIMBERLY CLARK CORPORATION

HOOVER SPIRIT VACUUM CLEANER, MODEL S3485

L ife is full of deep questions. Queries like "Why do chickens have wings if they can't fly?" are best left unvoiced, since some clown up in the Cosmic Quality Control department might overhear and say to himself, "Gee, I hadn't thought of that; we'd better do away with the wings," and then my fantastic chicken wing recipe would be utterly worthless. Others, like "Why does my Hoover Spirit vacuum cleaner feature Medium and Low suction settings?" and "Why would I ever want to use either of them instead of the High setting?" and "Isn't this all just a crock to make me think that Hoover has provided me with a fancy custom feature when the feature itself is actually worthless?" are less risky to pose, although no less vexing to ponder.

As it happens, these are precisely the questions I recently asked of a customer-service rep at Hoover. I had first consulted my owner's manual, which offered little guidance other than the self-justifying suggestion that the consumer "increase or decrease suction for various cleaning tasks." Yeah, okay, but *which* tasks? I mean, it's called a vacuum cleaner, right? When I turn it on, I want to create a *vacuum,* free of dirt, dust, and cat hairs, and that means I need maximum suction. So why would I ever want to dial it down to a lower setting?

"It's for vacuuming curtains, and maybe doilies," explained the well-mannered rep at Hoover. "If you knock it down to Low or Medium, you should be able to clean the fabric without sucking it up into the machine and clogging everything." I hadn't thought of this, so I dragged my Hoover out of the closet, wheeled it over to the one curtain in my apartment, and replaced the floor-cleaning attachment with the upholstery wand. Beginning with High suction, I tentatively swept the wand across the fabric. Sure enough, within a second or two a significant portion of the curtain had been sucked up into the suction hose and the vacuum motor was making unhappy noises. I turned off the machine, restored the curtain, changed the suction setting to Medium, and prepared to try again.

The
Hoover
Company

This was hardly an improvement. The curtain was soon bonding with the vacuum cleaner again, this time with such ardor that the curtain rod was actually yanked off of its brackets. There was a faint burning smell just as I turned the appliance off. My curtain, meanwhile, was a wrinkled mess and did not seem appreciably cleaner than when I'd started the whole misbegotten exercise. Twice bitten and thrice shy, I decided to forgo the Low setting. Nature may abhor a vacuum, but probably not as much as I did at that moment.

REAL-FUR MOUSE CAT TOY

A few years back I got Lizzie all the usual toys for Christmas: the catnip mouse, the wind-up mouse, the ball with the bell inside, the punching bag, and so on. So there I am, helping her unwrap them (she has little trouble with the tape) and, well, let's say she's not looking too enthused, if you know what I mean. She's giving me this look that says, "Yeah, yeah, the same old props, big fucking deal. Will you please feed me now?"

Then we unwrap the last one, something called a Real-Fur Mouse, and I'm actually embarrassed—it's got no catnip, no bell, it doesn't wind up and run around the room. It's just this very realistic-looking mouse. I only bought it because I thought it was cool to see a cat toy that looked like a *genuine rodent* instead of a cartoonish toy with huge ears and a ridiculously pointy nose. The fur is supposedly real meese-fleece, but who cares, right?

Vo-Toys, Inc.

Lizzie does. She goes berserk. Two days later, the other toys are still untouched and Mr. Real-Fur Mouse is shredded to bits, little tufts of his real fur scattered all over the apartment. Six years, two cats, and over a hundred mice later, I think we can safely say this product has earned *Inconspicuous Consumption*'s highest rating.

GLIDE DENTAL FLOSS, MINT FLAVOR, 50-METER SIZE

W e all know we're supposed to floss, but lots of us don't get around to it as often as we should. That might change, however, if more people become aware of Glide, the first dental floss I've encountered that makes flossing genuinely enjoyable.

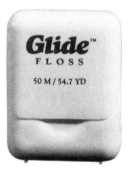

It all starts, as so many consumer pleasures do, with the packaging. Unlike most floss dispensers, which look like they took about five minutes to design, the Glide dispenser is clearly the product of some serious creative thought. With its attractively contoured curved edges and clever little "feet" at the base, the Glide package is a modernist treat that's extremely difficult to resist. If it's possible for dental floss to be seductive, then that's what this is.

And while most seductions promise more than they deliver, Glide only gets better as you go along. Pop open the appealingly angled lid and the true genius of the package is revealed: a small, tinted *window* providing a view into the dispenser's interior. In addition to letting you see precisely how much Glide you have left, this nifty little feature also allows you to watch the floss spool rotate as you

W. L. GORE & ASSOCIATES, INC.

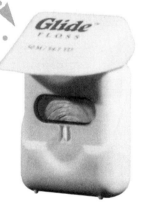

pull more Glide out of the dispenser, which looks very cool indeed.

Glide came to my attention via the enthusiastic recommendation of Gretchen Stoeltje of San Francisco, who describes the dispenser's curves as "voluptuous." She says Glide "is made of some undoubtedly toxic petroleum product that's just a whole lot smoother to floss with than waxed cotton, plus it tastes and smells exactly like Tic Tacs." She's right — Glide really does make for a more pleasant, less irritating flossing experience. Unlike normal floss, which tends to shred and leave behind little fibers when confronted with closely spaced teeth, Glide just, uh, glides right through even the tightest of dental crevices. It's also very easy on the gums. And the minty flavor *is* Tic Tac–esque.

As for the toxic-petroleum deal, I called W. L. Gore & Associates' consumer-response line and learned that Glide is actually made from a polymer called polytetrafluoroethylene, which has nothing to do with petroleum but happens to be the same stuff used in the company's Gore-Tex rainwear products. When I asked the phone rep if poly-whatsis might possibly be toxic, she responded, "Oh, heavens no. It's FDA-approved!" Now, when you consider that this is the same FDA that lets us eat such chemistry-class concoctions as Spam and Slim Jims, I can't call this a particularly effective vote of confidence. If I were W. L. Gore, I'd keep all the polymer info safely under wraps and play up the Tic Tac angle.

SCOTT BATHROOM TISSUE, 1000-SHEET ROLL ● ● ● ● ●

I just can't get too worked up over toilet paper. Oops, forgive me, how could I have been so crude — it's not *toilet paper,* it's *bathroom tissue.* And this one's softer than that one, and this one's quilted, and that one's multiply, and this one over here is more absorbent, and that one over there has little air pockets built into each sheet, blah-blah-blah.

Please. No matter how you dress it up, toilet paper still boils down to the stuff we use to wipe the crap from our butts, and no amount of clever packaging or marketing is going to change that. In the final analysis, TP offers next to nothing in terms of consumer satisfaction. Oh, I suppose you could get a few hours of entertainment debating the respective merits of the under-the-bottom vs. the over-the-top methods of hanging the roll (try me), but even that wears thin eventually. There's a reason why college students who've moved off-campus all sneak back into their dorms to steal TP from the supply closet: everyone, from the consumptively challenged to the supermarket-savvy, realizes there's no residual consumer tingle associated with the purchase of this product. Surely even the most ardent critic of big government would agree that in a better, more progressive world, TP would simply be made available to us free of charge at municipal drop-off sites.

All of which brings me to my supermarket's paper goods aisle. I'd grabbed a few rolls of paper towels and a pack of napkins, but was having difficulty locating ScotTissue, my usual brand of TP. Then I realized I was staring right at it, only the package design used on the individual rolls had been changed. The wrapper's familiar ribbon-and-bow motif had been replaced by a generic-looking cloud-and-wave design. The interesting part was in the upper-left corner, where a burst contained a little illustration of the *old* design, along with the following caption: "Still the Original!"

I'd never seen anything like this. Why introduce a new design if you're just going to spike it with a rendering of the old design? Was Scott attempting to have it both ways, trying to woo new consumers into the fold while reassuring old customers who might be turned off by the switcheroo? I got on the phone and chatted with a friendly rep at the Scott consumer relations department to find out.

"When you change the package," she said, "a lot of times people get confused or think you're changing the product. We want people to know the inside product is exactly the same." The little notice with the old design would eventually be eliminated, she said.

If you think I'm the only one who takes this stuff seriously, think again. The rep said the new design, which had been introduced about a month prior to our discussion, had kept her phone in a near-constant state of ringing. "There are a lot of mixed emotions about it," she said. "Some people like it; we've had a few people who said they'll never buy the product again. It's definitely something that's shaken up the consumer." Which, in the case of TP, couldn't have happened a moment too soon.

CRAYOLA MAGIC SCENT CRAYONS, 16-PACK

Crayola, a brand name no American child can avoid or escape, hadn't been on my mind for years until my friend Andrea gave me a box of an amazing product: Crayola Magic Scent Crayons. If you hold these crayons up to your nose, they just smell like crayons. But if you color with them and then smell the paper, your nostrils are flooded with familiar scents.

Each Magic Scent crayon has its own unique bouquet. Technically speaking, these crayons are known by their scents rather than their colors. The green Magic Scent crayon is called pine, not green, and the red crayon is called rose. And sure enough, that's what they smell like. A few of the other

varieties, like baby powder (white) and soap (lavender), are as clever as they are fragrant.

Some of the other scents, however, are not quite what you'd expect from a kid's product. The logical smell for the black crayon, for instance, would be licorice. Instead they've called it *leather jacket*, which is either completely brilliant or totally fucked, depending on my mood. Either way, it isn't the sort of wholesome, child-oriented pitch I'd expect from Crayola. Other Magic Scents that lean toward the imaginative include smoke (gray), lumber (tan), the frighteningly realistic-smelling dirt (brown), and —brace yourself—*new car* (blue, although it seems like almost any color would do). Is this product really intended for kids?

"Sure it is," maintained Crayola spokesperson Sandy Horner, who said the company regularly solicits input from all-kids focus groups. As she also explained, the original edition of Magic Scents, introduced in the summer of '94, was much more food-centric—the black crayon *was* licorice, and other scents in the series included bubble gum (pink), blueberry (blue), cherry (dark red), banana (yellow), and so on. But after parents began voicing concerns that their kids might be tempted to eat the food-scented crayons, Crayola decided to update the product about a year later. White changed from coconut to baby powder; purple went from grape to lilac; orange switched from orange to tulip; and brown, which had been designated as chocolate, became dirt. (The big irony there, of course, is that most little kids like eating dirt almost as much as they like eating chocolate.)

You'd think that having to overhaul a product so soon

after its launch would be a corporate embarrassment, but Horner tried to stay positive. "We like to replenish our products," she said. "We needed new smells to keep the excitement going." Horner's own excitement level, however, is not without its limits—the dirt crayon, she admitted, "makes me gag," and "the lilac one really grosses me out."

One really has to wonder how many sales of this product are coming from adults, especially since most of my friends have been totally fascinated when I've shown them Magic Scents. (The best reaction, from my friend Liz: "If I mix new car with smoke, I'll get rental car!") All of which leads to the obvious notion of adults-only Magic Scents. It isn't hard to envision the fragrance listing for an X-rated version of this product, and I'd personally stand on line to buy Magic Scents with a white-trash or tavern or gas station theme. Now if we could just place a few grown-ups in those focus groups . . .

GREEN BAY PACKERS UNIFORMS

D evotion to a professional sports team is among the more curious examples of brand loyalty in our culture. And if the team is the product, then uniforms function as the package design. Moreover, for those of us who enjoy watching steroid-pumped morons chasing a little ball for millions of dollars, uniform design is a crucial element in our visual landscape. And believe me, with the current trend of using "contemporary" colors like purple and teal, not to mention the optical minefield posed by such uniform blights as double-knits and ignorant baseball players who don't know how to wear their stirrups properly, things are looking pretty grim out there.

Football uniforms should be the easiest of all to design—the team names and logos don't appear on the jerseys, so there's no room for misguided creativity or botched typographic experiments. All you have to do is put together a decent color combination and a reasonably attractive helmet. It therefore amazes me how some teams still manage to mess this up—go on, just *try* to watch a Cincinnati Bengals game without wincing.

It is with these failures in mind that we turn to the Green Bay Packers, whose uniforms provide a soothing balm to retina-weary sports fans and sharp-eyed product aesthetes alike. It all turns on one of history's great color schemes: a rich, deep green for the jerseys (officially spec'd as PMS 553 for licensing purposes), a nice mustard yellow for the pants and helmets (PMS 116), and white for the trim and detailing. Throw in a few splashes of brown (the football), black (the antiglare charcoal under the quarterback's eyes), and red (a bit of blood on the linebacker's forearm), and you've got a primary/secondary color feast. It may not sound like much, but on a brisk November day you can pick 11 players—*any* 11 players—dress them up in the Pack's gorgeous autumnal hues, plop them down on a gridiron, and sit back and admire the whole tableau with tears of joy in your long-suffering eyes.

AUTHENTIC-REALISTIC SNAKE TOY, INDETERMINATE SPECIES

I f you want to see just how misguided an "educational" toy can be, take a look at the packaging on an Authentic-Realistic snake, a rubber reptile toy manufactured in China. Like lots of foreign products made for quick export to the American cheap-merchandise market, Authentic-Realistic snakes feature ad copy that's so incredibly bad, it borders on the brilliant.

It all starts on the front of the package, right beneath the Authentic-Realistic brand name, where it says the toy will "help you know more to the natural," an odd turn of a phrase that sounds like it was meant to promote a nudist colony. Things get even more interesting on the back of the package, where the manufacturer helpfully runs photos of all six snake species available in the Authentic-Realistic series, each accompanied by a description that will probably set zoology back a few decades. Herewith a few of the highlights, with typos and grammatical manglings left intact:

* "The Cuban racer snake are found in Cuba. Usually they are overhanging around on the trees. When they see the target, they move very fast and quick to hunt. They can eat rat, small birds and the small active objects."

* "[Garter snakes] frequently be found in streams and ponds. Also, they are found in desert country follow the courses of streams and riuers . . ."

* "The slender tail of a two foot adult [pygmy rattlesnake] terminates in a diminutive rattle that can scarcely by heard at a distance of six feet. . . . The pygmy rattlesnake would be a very nangerous snake indeed."

Uh, right. Unfortunately, the product itself doesn't look like any of the snake species shown on the package, so I can't tell which variety it is. I eventually tied its head and upper body to a doorknob in my apartment and let its tail hang down toward the floor. My cat Barbarella soon made short work of it, which just shows that some of the small active objects are more nangerous than others.

THREE

STRANGE

If necessity is the mother of invention, as the saying goes, then one need only glance around the consumer landscape to conclude that there must be some very odd necessities running around out there. The products that follow—some silly, some quite commendable—offer a telling reminder that human ingenuity knows no limitations, least of all the limitation of so-called common sense.

Call me crazy, but when my socks lose their elasticity and sag down toward my ankles, I figure it's time to buy new socks. If my underwear starts riding up my butt, I figure I've bought the wrong size, they've shrunk in the wash, or I need to lose some weight. If my shirttails begin to come loose, I figure I must not have tucked them in properly.

This all sounds sensible to me, but not to the folks at BeautiControl Cosmetics, a Texas mail-order house. They have a simple solution for clothes that won't stay put: *glue* them into place.

That solution comes in the form of Body Glue, a water-soluble adhesive packaged in a roll-on applicator. If your bra strap insists on flopping down or the lower edge of your bathing suit bottom is riding up, just roll a little Body Glue

onto the pertinent body area, press the garment to your skin, sit still for three minutes, and then go out and face the world brimming with, uh, confidence. You should soon be feeling confident enough to be adhering all sorts of clothing and accessories to yourself. According to the literature on the package, Body Glue is ideal for use on shoulder pads, collars, cuffs, slips, bustiers, wigs and toupees, strapless dresses, and even earrings.

BEAUTICONTROL COSMETICS, INC.

I wanted to take this product for a test drive, but I tend not to have too many shifting-clothes problems. So instead I just applied some Body Glue to my forehead and stuck a smallish piece of fabric there. Sure enough, it stayed put, and continued to do so as I spent the next half hour feeding the cats, checking my E-mail, emptying the dishwasher, and so on. I could have accomplished the same thing with a piece of Scotch tape or a glue stick, though, which makes you wonder how much Body Glue the BeautiControl people can be selling at $25 a pop. But for those who truly want to bond with their wardrobes, here's a way to be tacky in two ways at once.

CAR JOHN DISPOSABLE URINAL

I t is a matter of no minor serendipity that a book devoted to inconspicuous consumption should review a product devoted to inconspicuous excretion. You don't have to be a fan of the scatological to appreciate the warped genius behind the Car John, which, as its name implies, is designed to provide relief for the automobile-bound male whose bladder is about to burst. It's a Port-a-Pot that fits in your glove compartment.

Essentially a vinyl pouch with a cylindrical nozzle, the Car John is a worthy attempt to build a better mousetrap, but I'm afraid it's not completely successful. For starters, you need to park your car in order to use it. Why not invent something that would facilitate urination while still driving? Now that would be progress.

Perhaps more to the point, since when did the side of the road, the woods, the bushes, and large roadkill become unacceptable cover for answering nature's call? Anticipating this response on the part of the consumer, the Car

BRICE
CREATIONS

John promotes itself as the ideal option for "potentially dangerous neighborhoods," where dashing out of the car for roadside relief might be a dicey proposition. It's been my experience, however, that the more dangerous the neighborhood, the more likely the locals are to be pissing in the streets anyway, therefore obviating the need for the Car John. I mean, seriously, did you ever try to take a roadside leak in Beverly Hills? *That's* where this thing might come in handy.

Other concerns: Women are no doubt wondering what this product has to offer them, and I'm sorry to report that the answer appears to be "not much" — the Car John offers no female-oriented attachment, and as of yet there's no such thing as a Car Jane. One might also question the merits of marketing a product whose primary audience is obviously drunken drivers, but I guess it's important to remember that vehicular homicidists are people too.

On the positive side, the Car John's instructions and accompanying promotional literature offer a litany of urinary hilarity. One of the more inspired bits touts the product's nonautomotive potential: "Of course the Car John can be used outside the car. With a 'privacy cover' (a newspaper, coat, etc.), it can be used almost anywhere. Naturally, one would seek out a secluded area, such as a telephone booth." I always wondered what Superman was doing in there. Although the packaging describes the Car John as "disposable," a little note on the pouch implores the user, "Protect your environment — do not throw away. Seal it, take it home and empty it. It can be rinsed, cleaned and used again." And really, this makes perfect sense — you don't throw away the cat box when you change the litter, right? Like so many well-intentioned attempts at providing a genuine public service, the Car John is slightly imperfect, but in a society dying to relieve itself in every way possible, it's a noble attempt to give us everything but the graffiti on the bathroom walls.

"SWEET SUE" FEMALE TORSO MODEL

Way cooler than an anatomically correct inflatable doll and niftier than the cover of Nirvana's *In Utero* album, Sweet Sue is your basic science-class model of the human female. When she arrives fresh from the warehouse, she's just another au naturel plastic doll — 18 inches high, nice smile, no arms or legs (just like the Venus de Milo!). Remove her detachable breastplate, however, and you find Sue is a lot more woman than you ever suspected. Residing in her torso are a dozen removable organs, including her liver, pancreas, spleen, lungs, intestines, and heart, all painted in medically correct colors.

Occasionally I like to take out the organs and play with them, but more often I prefer just to leave them in place, exposed for all to see. Sue doesn't mind — she's blessed with that rarest of attributes, inner beauty, and as such is *proud* of her body and comfortable with its display.

As her impeccable posture, artfully applied makeup, and Hillary-esque headband attest, she's also the product of a world-class finishing school. No, the organ you're most curious about is *not* included, but my friend Romy observes that Sue has "a nice butt," and she couldn't be more right.

ANATOMICAL CHART COMPANY

A close second to Brenda Starr in the dream-date sweepstakes, Sue is among the more expensive items reviewed in this book ($100 plus shipping), and worth every last penny.

FUN KIST PLASTIC MISTLETOE

I like Christmas and I like kissing, so it makes sense that I also like mistletoe. When I'm honest with myself, however, I admit something that most of you already know: mistletoe is a rather ugly little weed. What's more, it's usually available only in limp little sprigs that are anything but romantic, and if your apartment is as overheated as most of mine have been, you've no doubt discovered that it takes only a day or two for even the most robust mistletoe to be reduced to a dried-out twig, littering its leaves all over the floor.

None of this was specifically on my mind when I wandered into Woolworth's one day in search of assorted Christmas provisions. I got a stocking for my sweetie, some glitter and lights, and was about to join a very long checkout line when I spied the Fun Kist Plastic Mistletoe. A cursory inspection confirmed that this product is actually better than the real thing: an attractive, bell-shaped bunch of greenery, nice leaf-to-berry ratio, a tasteful red bow tied onto the primary stem, and a cleverly camouflaged hook for hanging the whole assemblage over your chosen spot for Yuletide necking. Sturdy, durable, and ready to see you through any number of holiday seasons, it looks absolutely convincing

SCHUSTERS OF TEXAS, INC.

56

from even a short distance away. If your ceilings are high enough, nobody'll be able to tell the difference even if they're standing right underneath it. And trust me—it works its smooching magic as well as the real thing.

SAFE-T-MAN

A perfect gift for paranoiacs and lonely hearts alike, Safe-T-Man is a life-sized doll designed to "trick people into thinking you have the protection of a male guardian." Or, to put it another way, he's the one car passenger who'll never be accused of backseat driving.

Safe-T-Man is quite the trickster. He's designed to look like he's 175 pounds, but he weighs in at only four; he stands 5'10" tall, but his elongated trunk makes him look like a six-footer when you prop him up in the passenger seat or your apartment window. Deception is so central to his function that he's actually described as a "simulated male."

This description, along with Safe-T-Man himself, comes from the Safety Zone catalog, a mail-order operation dealing in alarm systems, self-defense gadgets, and similar exploitations of white suburban fear. Noting that "You're never alone with Safe-T-Man," they offer this oversized Ken doll for a very safe-sounding $119.95 (that's $30 a pound—you'd get better value buying steak). For $34.95 more, you can procure a Safe-T-Man Tote Bag, ideal for storing Safe-T-Man when he's not in use. Oh, and you'll also need a clothing budget—although Safe-T-Man is shown wearing a jogging suit over a red turtleneck in the Safety Zone catalog, he is shipped *sans* wardrobe, allowing you to "dress him according to your own preferences."

THE SAFETY ZONE

Visually, Safe-T-Man bears a strong resemblance to a 1970s version of *Jeopardy!* host Alex Trebeck. His mustache looks pretty cheesy, and I have a feeling there's a very good reason why the Safety Zone people put sunglasses on him for all the catalog photos. None of which is to suggest that Safe-T-Man might not be a better conversationalist than your in-laws or a better date than most of the people who run personal ads. Plus I'm sure there's a bad movie just waiting to be written about Safe-T-Man, and I'd love to be his agent when the studios come sniffing around, but so far he hasn't returned my calls.

THE ENEMY WIND, VHS VIDEOCASSETTE

I f porno flicks offend your personal sensibilities and snuff films seem completely beyond the pale, don't worry. I've got just the thing to give you that voyeuristic, VCR-driven rush without offending even the most PC of dispositions. And the unlikely purveyor of this small-screen stimulation is none other than the much-maligned Weather Channel.

To explain: I have a limitless fascination with the raw power and natural beauty of tornadoes. By happy coincidence, our nation's midwestern region features a limitless supply of kamikaze simps whose first instinct upon seeing a twister is to run directly toward it with a camcorder. Assuming the videographer survives the whole ordeal, this sort of tape inevitably finds its way to the Weather Channel.

The Enemy Wind is a 45-minute compendium of such footage, with some junior-high meteorology lessons and civil defense warnings thrown in to give the project some semblance of "educational" validity. That crap doesn't fool me, though — the science-related sequences repeatedly give way to incredible shots of tornadoes being born, tornadoes slicing through small towns, big tornadoes spinning off little tornadoes, tornadoes dancing their way across the Kansas-Oklahoma border, tornadoes heading straight for the guy with the camera, and so on. Believe me, it's *way* more intense than anything in *Twister*. The fact of the matter is that lots of people totally get off on watching tornadoes, and the Weather Channel knows it. That's why they're selling this video to begin with. When the network runs a house ad touting the tape, it's the swank tornadic action that's prominently featured, not the Meteorology 111 stuff.

When I mentioned *The Enemy Wind* to my friend John, he flashed a big smile of understanding and quipped, "Sure, weather-porn." As it turns out, the tape's overall effect *is* remarkably pornographic. Just like with a porn film, dialogue and plot are irrelevant — just give me better focus on that close-up shot, please. Just like with a porn film, I fast-forward past the boring bits to get to the good parts and rewind to watch them again. Just like with a porn film, the use of amateur video footage enhances the *vérité* feel of the scene. And finally, just like with a porn film, I find myself mumbling, "Ohmygod, ohmygod, ohmygod" and "Holy shit, holy fucking shit." Want to take the comparison even further? That moment when the funnel cloud touches down functions nicely as a money shot, and the thought of the cameraman being ripped to shreds adds a tasty snuff element.

THE WEATHER CHANNEL

At $23.90, including shipping, *The Enemy Wind* is admittedly a bit pricier than a trip to the corner vid shop to rent *Dirty Debutantes #22*, and has an even lamer title to boot. But the thought that some poor fool risked his life to film a twister when he should've been hiding in the storm cellar along with everyone else — all so you could watch the carnage from the comfort of your living room — is worth the price of admission right there. Plus you won't have to waste time wondering how many of the cast members are sporting breast implants.

666 COLD PREPARATION WITH QUININE, 4-OUNCE BOTTLE

I'd heard about it, I'd read about it, someone had even sent me a photograph of it. Somewhere in our vast consumer landscape lurked a product too perfect to believe, a product whose very name promised hours of amusement. Somewhere out there was a bottle of 666 Cold Preparation with my name on it.

Yes, 666. As in the mark of the beast. As in the sign of the devil. As in one very busy public relations department back at the manufacturer's home office, or so I figured. Remember all the fuss back in the eighties when some crackpots decided the Procter & Gamble logo was some kind of secret pagan symbol? There were angry letters and phone calls, talk show appearances, threats of boycotts, threats of *bombings*, the works. And that was over an innocuous little illustration. What would the clean-living crowd make of something that explicitly called itself 666? You might as well go all the way and call your product Lucifer's Jism or something like that. Assuming that the 666 name wasn't being hyped or promoted for its novelty potential — and my scouts assured me that it was not — this appeared to have all the makings of a very entertaining consumer experience.

Just one problem: I couldn't find the stuff. None of my contacts who'd seen it had bothered to buy a bottle, and nobody could recall who the manufacturer was. Some guy in

MONTICELLO DRUG COMPANY

Kansas promised to send me some but never followed through. Someone else said he thought he'd seen Jay Leno do a 666 routine but couldn't remember when. Inquiries at my neighborhood drugstores were met, predictably, with very confused looks.

Then, finally, I spotted 666 at the supermarket, on a shelf full of old-fashioned remedies. Blithely ignoring the potential for eternal damnation, I examined my long-coveted prize. It looked like your basic bottle of snake oil, complete with a vaguely retro package design and some dubious claims of medicinal prowess. Aside from the product name itself, the whole Mephistophelian angle was entirely absent: the actual "666" typography was presented without a hint of either irony or menace. I proudly displayed the bottle in the upper compartment of my shopping cart and tried not to worry about devilish implications when the product's bar code failed to register properly in the supermarket's electronic checkout scanning system.

The manufacturer, as it turned out, was a Florida firm called the Monticello Drug Company. Things got positively surreal when a quick call to directory assistance revealed their phone number to be 904-384-3666. By this time I was practically pinching myself to be sure this wasn't some sort of inconspicuously consumptive fantasy. Working myself into a lather of utterly inauthentic Christian outrage, I dashed off a letter of complaint to Monticello, suggesting that they "owe an explanation to God-fearing

666
PREPARATION
WITH
QUININE
For Relief of Headache,
Body Aches and Pains, and
Fever due to Colds.
SAFETY SEALED CAP.
DO NOT USE IF IMPRINTED NECKBAND AROUND
CAP IS BROKEN OR MISSING.
DISTRIBUTOR
Monticello Drug Company
Jacksonville, Florida 32202
4 FLUID OZ. (118 ml.)

consumers like myself." Then I sat back and waited for the inevitable form-letter response.

A week passed, and then another, with nary a reply from Monticello. Convinced that Beelzebub had intercepted my letter, I got on the phone and chatted with Monticello Vice President Tracey Fore, who explained that the product name dates back to 1890, when the company's founder, a Florida pharmacist named Tharp Roberts, came up with the 666 formula.

"Back in those days," said Fore, "you didn't go to a doctor unless your arm was chopped off or something like that. If you were just sick, you went down to the drugstore to see your pharmacist." Roberts, said Fore, made and peddled a variety of tonics and elixirs for his customers, but it was his formula number 666 that proved most popular. In 1908, he went commercial and began distributing the product, primarily in the South, where it remains a popular brand today.

Fore acknowledged that Monticello is aware of the whole biblical issue but insisted it isn't that big a deal. "It obviously has nothing to do with any demonic reference," he said. "Down here, we're a well-known brand name." To my surprise, he said the company receives less than a dozen letters per year on the matter. (My own inquiry apparently had been lost in the mail.)

Meanwhile, almost overlooked in the shuffle was a question of tangential but undeniable relevance: does the stuff actually work? Fore said he uses 666 himself but is well aware that modern medicine has yet to cure the common cold. "If you have a cold, nothing's going to make it go away," he admitted. "But our formula can make you as comfortable as the next guy's. Maybe a little bit more."

Fore's candor was admirable, but was it really just a netherworldly ruse designed to lull me into a false sense of complacency? I feared it would be some time before I'd find out, since I rarely get colds myself—maybe once every two years or so. But whether by benign coincidence or Satanic machination, no sooner did 666 enter my home than I came down with a whopper case of sneezing, sniffling, coughing, and so on. I'd exhausted all the usual remedies—aspirin, chicken soup, vats of OJ, Sudafed, booze, *Fawlty Towers* tapes, whining phone chats with loved ones—when I noticed the bottle of 666 beckoning from across the room.

Why not? I opened the bottle and pierced the interior safety seal; no astral demons appeared to escape. Still cautious, I brought the open bottle up to my malfunctioning nose and took as good a whiff as my cold would allow. Seemed harmless enough. So I poured out a tablespoonful, held my breath for a moment, and gulped it down.

Within nanoseconds of the potion's arrival upon my taste buds, the real explanation for the 666 name became apparent—if hellfire could be distilled into liquid form, surely this is what it would taste like. As for its effectiveness as a remedy, I'll say this for 666: after one serving, my cold felt like the least of my problems.

THE "YOUNG ONE"

Y ou don't have to be an antiabortion yahoo to get a kick out of the "Young One," an actual-size plastic model of an 11- to 12-week-old fetus, although I suppose it wouldn't hurt. Intended for distribution at churches, schools, doctors' offices, social service agencies, and, of course, abortion clinics, the "Young One" (for some reason it's always in quotes) is one of the pro-life lobby's more interesting PR tools. You have to admit it's certainly preferable to, say, shooting up a clinic with an automatic rifle.

The point behind the "Young One," of course, is to make us realize how closely a fetus (or "preborn baby," as the model's purveyors like to say) resembles an adult. Just in case you can't figure this out for yourself, a little card accompanying the "Young One" features a laundry list of familiar points to drive the message home: "Heart is beating. He squints, swallows, and can make a fist. He has fingerprints. He is sensitive to heat, touch, light, and noise. He sucks his thumb." And so on. All of which is fine, except that when I look at the "Young One," with his oversized head and fetal pose, I don't think of his similarity to you and me; I think of the more bizarro scenes toward the end of Kubrick's *2001*, which probably is not what the Project "Young One" folks had in mind.

PROJECT "YOUNG ONE," INC.

I'm fairly certain there are some other things they didn't have in mind either, such as my discovery that you can adapt your "Young One" to suit your needs. The little guys are just the right size and weight to make excellent Christmas tree ornaments, for example. And while the model's accompanying literature claims that the "Young One" has been a very successful antiabortion tool, thereby demonstrating that "God has unique ways to save His children," my two felines' enthusiastic reaction to this product shows that God also provides us with some irresistible cat toys just when we're least expecting it.

Although the "Young One" was designed to influence life-and-death issues, he comes on the cheap: small quantities will set you back just 30 cents per "Young One," and a graduated discount schedule knocks the price down to 22 cents a pop for 10,000 or more models. Best of all, by writing to Project "Young One," you'll get on the mailing list for a bunch of really awful and really entertaining propaganda at no extra charge.

GOD'S ARMOUR

They say you'll never have reason to fear if you keep the Lord close to your heart. This is now truer than ever thanks to God's Armour, a small, hardbound version of the New Testament with an interesting twist: the cover is *bulletproof*.

I always thought the mere presence of a Bible — even a torn and tattered version — was supposed to provide divine protection, but the folks behind God's Armour aren't taking any chances. The 3-by-4.5-inch book (whose name is derived from Ephesians 6:11: "Put on the whole armour of god, that ye may be able to stand against the wiles of the devil") can repel a .38-caliber bullet. And while God's Armour's diminutive dimensions obviously make it a poor substitute for a full-sized bulletproof vest, it's just the right size to slip unobtrusively into your chest pocket. If you'd rather protect your flank, God's Armour feels as natural in your back pants pocket as a well-worn wallet.

I suppose God's Armour might slightly increase your odds of surviving for more than five minutes in, say, Bosnia, Chechnya, or South Central Los Angeles, but it's not really intended as a self-defense tool. The people at Innovative Marketing Alliance, living up to their name, see God's Armour as a gift item, an ideal stocking stuffer for the 8.5 million uniformed Americans whose jobs sometimes put them in harm's way. According to the product's promo lit, God's Armour "allows families and friends of police, firefighters, military [personnel], or any uniformed service to say, 'I care' in a new and special way . . . [and] to communicate a very unique message."

It's interesting to ponder just what this unique message

INNOVATIVE
MARKETING
ALLIANCE

might be. After all, while nobody wants to see someone else get shot, most of us aren't so blunt as to bring up the issue in the first place. Giving your uniformed loved one a "normal" Bible, it seems to me, is like saying, "Here, just in case you need a little extra spiritual protection"; giving someone God's Armour, on the other hand, says, "Here, just in case you're slow on the draw or you run out of bullets or you're hopelessly outnumbered or your corrupt partner sells you out to the local crack dealer or your gun accidentally goes off or you square off against a bunch of Montana militiamen or you're innocently caught in the crossfire during a gang war." Oh, gee — thanks.

Incidentally, it turns out that God's Armour has an ideological ancestor in the not-so-distant past. Back in World War II, soldiers often carried Bibles with hefty brass covers, leading to a boatload of stories (many clearly apocryphal) about the metal-bound tomes deflecting the occasional bullet or bit of shrapnel. Of course, God's Armour also fits into a more timeless tradition: as someone once remarked, Jesus saves.

CREAMY HEAD, 8-OUNCE BOTTLE

If you're in the market for some good head — and who isn't? — you might want to get yourself a bottle of Creamy Head, a foaming agent designed to add a layer of suds to mixed drinks. Or, as the label on the bottle imaginatively puts it, "Creamy Head, for a creamy head on cocktail shaker drinks." With a product name as good as this one, I guess they figured they might as well repeat it as often as possible.

On the Creamy Head label is a painstakingly staged photo of a good-sized cocktail — a whiskey sour, looks like —

with a nice, fluffy-looking head. I've shown this photo to a number of acquaintances, and everyone agrees that the foam on top definitely makes the drink look more desirable. Now, why is that? We all like to see a nice head on a glass of beer, of course — that's how we know it hasn't gone flat — but why do we respond so positively to a head on a drink with no carbonated elements? The head, apparently, is one of those inconspicuous details that push our internal buttons.

In search of further enlightenment, I brought Creamy Head to my local bartender, Patrick O'Connor. "Oh yeah, I've seen stuff like this," he said. "We used to use a different brand, called Frothy. It's mostly egg whites."

ROMANOFF INTERNATIONAL, INC.

Actually, Creamy Head is mostly water and chemicals, at least according to the ingredients listing, which includes propylene glycol, polysorbate 80, sorbitol, and potassium sorbate. No mention of egg whites, but maybe they just forgot.

Whatever's in there, it works. While I have yet to try Creamy Head in a mixed drink, I have found that four dashes of this product, along with some vigorous shaking action, turn a glass of tap water into something that looks more like dishwater. The taste and smell are nil, and the absence of any nutrition info on the label leads me to believe there's no such info to report, all of which means that Creamy Head is one of those unique consumer goods: it adds that special something, even though the product itself is essentially nothing.

NIPPLESS, 6-PACK

O ne of the simplest yet most intriguing items to come my way is Nippless, a woman's product of Japanese origin. Like so many Japanese goods, this one features a beautiful package design: a two-piece cardboard packet, 4.5 inches wide by 3 inches long, with a plastic hinge at the lower-left corner that allows the festively ornamented upper piece to swing away, revealing the die-cut lower piece. Inside this lower section are six pairs of small, round, flesh-colored adhesive appliqués, each about an inch and a half wide, that look very much like Band-Aids. The idea is for women to wear these on their breasts when they want to go braless but don't want their nipples or areolae to show through a light-colored T-shirt or blouse. How's *that* for form following function?

I initially thought Nippless deserved high points on the weirdness scale, but several of my female friends say the overall concept is nothing new — apparently women's magazines have long recommended using Band-Aids to achieve the same effect. But the ability of the Japanese to come up with a specialized product for this narrowly targeted purpose shows how thoroughly they've beaten us at our own consumer capitalist game. This is the sort of product-development acumen every country should strive for.

Nippless was brought to my attention by my neighbor Keira, who declined to wear them in public but reports that they held up quite well when she applied them at room temperature and then stood in front of her open freezer, a quality-control test of her own devising. But my pal Andrea says that when she subjected Nippless to a similar nipple-erection trial in front of her air

MANUFACTURER
UNCERTAIN

conditioner, the product began to peel off around the edges. Andrea, who initially agreed to test-drive Nippless in public, changed her mind after deciding the rondelles looked "ridiculous" when worn beneath a white T-shirt. (She later added that Nippless hurts like hell when peeled off.)

Lots of Japanese package designs feature smatterings of inadvertently entertaining English, and Nippless is no exception. The front of the package says, "For swimming, dancing, and T-shirt time," along with, "Please put it on your bust." How polite. There's also some significant irony lurking within the product name itself. While *Nippless* is obviously meant to connote *Nipple-less*, some of our more politically incorrect consumers might simply separate the word into its component syllables —*Nip-less*—and interpret it as a racist call to arms against, of all people, the Japanese. Which just goes to show that maybe they haven't completely mastered this consumer capitalist thing after all.

THIRSTY DOG! AND THIRSTY CAT!, 1-LITER BOTTLES

T ap water? You're still giving your pet tap water?" So reads the incredulous headline on the promotional flier for Thirsty Dog! and Thirsty Cat!, whose manufacturers are convinced they can give America's pet owners a major case of the guilts. And why not? I already feel pretty guilty about the way I treat my cats: I don't play with them often enough, I don't let them go outside even when they stare plaintively out the window in that cat-in-a-gilded-cage sort of way, and when I go to work every morning they give me The Look —that incredibly potent combination of cuteness and sadness that says, "And now you're gonna just *leave* us here?" The Look, which Lizzie and

Barbarella have perfected, sends me trudging off to the subway feeling like a total shit.

And now, on top of everything else, it turns out I've been serving up the beverage equivalent of raw sewage in their water dish. At least that's what the folks at the Original Pet Drink Co. would have me believe. Tap water, you see, is riddled with impurities, trace elements, and additives, which is why it's only fit for lower beasts like you and me. Our pets deserve better.

And better is just what Thirsty Dog! and Thirsty Cat! are designed to be. The two pet drinks, which come in one-liter bottles and retail for $1.79, are made from purified water, fortified with a long list of vitamins and minerals, and are — get this — *carbonated,* making them the Perrier, rather than the Evian, of the four-legged set. Each comes in a flavor designed for maximum appeal with its respective animal market — Tangy Fish for Thirsty Cat! and Crispy Beef for Thirsty Dog! (I'm still puzzling over the latter — a "crispy" drink?). According to the promo lit, 15,000 palatability tests showed that 70 percent of animals given a choice preferred the bottled stuff over tap water.

For the record, I tried Thirsty Cat! myself and thought it tasted like mediocre seltzer. I was pretty sure Barbarella would like it anyway — she likes everything — but Lizzie provided a more interesting test case. Lizzie exhibits, among other peculiarities, a remarkable lack of interest in drinking. She eats only canned food, not dry, and this apparently provides her all the moisture she needs. Over the course of ten years, I've seen her take three, maybe four laps out of the water dish. She doesn't drink from the toilet bowl, and she even turns up her nose at milk.

So I figured this gave Thirsty Cat! a chance to score a major coup. If Lizzie would down this product, I'd look into buying stock in the company.

Unfortunately, four days' worth of Thirsty Cat! did not transform Lizzie into a thirsty cat. She stuck to her usual routine — eating, sleeping, visiting the litter box, and so on. As for Barbarella, I wasn't really paying as much attention to her, but I assumed she was drinking the stuff. Meanwhile, I just refilled the dish with fresh Thirsty Cat! each day.

Then, on the morning of the fifth day, I came out of the shower and found Barbarella in the bathroom sink, frantically lapping up every stray droplet of water she could find. Curious, I scooped her up, carried her to the kitchen, and plopped her down in front of the Thirsty Cat! bowl; she scampered away. So I replaced it with a bowl of tap water, tracked down Barbarella again (now lapping up water in the shower stall), and tried once more. After a few tentative sniffs, she tore into it, draining half the bowl in one sitting. In one sense, at least, Thirsty Cat! had lived up to its name.

LAWN MAKEUP AEROSOL SPRAY, 10.5-OUNCE CAN

The classic American fantasy of the perfectly manicured suburban lawn, which already supports the fertilizer, sprinkler, mower, garden hose, herbicide, and weed-whacker industries, has spawned a new product: Lawn Makeup, an aerosol spray. Lawn Makeup is sort of a last resort, something to reach for if the fertilizer, the sprinkler, the herbicide, and all the rest have failed you. It's basically a can of green spray paint designed for use on patches of brown, scorched lawn.

Lawn Makeup, whose inventors were probably inspired

by those infomercials for spray-on hair, is one of those ridiculously perfect products that sets off a series of very specific images in my brain: I see a suburban street lined with houses, each with an identical husband carefully spraying Lawn Makeup all over the front yard; I see the wives watching the husbands through the screen door, shaking their heads in disbelief but unable to resist yelling, "Honey, you missed a spot!"; I see the husbands looking back at the wives with annoyance before dutifully spraying the specified area; at this point I notice that the husbands all look exactly like Alan Arkin, which is scary enough to bring me back to reality.

My can of Lawn Makeup is marked "Palm Green"; other shades available include Cedar Green, Spring Green, and Kentucky Blue. The can features several other entertaining tidbits as well—I'm particularly fond of the boast that Lawn Makeup is *virtually* non-toxic" (emphasis mine), as well as the instructions to "spray a test area for color match," just like on the directions on fabric-dye packages. As a crowning touch, the manufacturers list the "ideal weather conditions" for using Lawn Makeup: "calm, warm, 68 degrees, and dry." Uh, guys, if the temperature's only up to 68, chances are my lawn isn't scorched in the first place.

GLOBAL
STAR PRODUCTS

But I shouldn't harp on the negative. In the spirit of giving credit where it's due, there's no denying that Lawn Makeup provides a plausible answer to an age-old question: if you've been wondering why the grass is always greener on the other side of the fence, here's the explanation.

ALL-WEATHER PAINTSTIK LIVESTOCK MARKER, 2.25-OUNCE STICK

A s long as we're on the subject of pigment application, this seems like a good time to discuss the All-Weather Paintstik, a product used by livestock farmers looking for an easy way to mark their herds. You say you don't have the time or the stomach to use the branding iron on ol' Bessie? Not to worry—just use the Paintstik to put your specialized mark on her.

The Paintstik, which is available in 11 colors (mine is blue), does an admirable job of distilling its specialized purpose into an utterly simple form: at four inches long by an inch wide, it looks very much like a big piece of chalk.

Strictly speaking, of course, it's really just another writing implement, ultimately taking its place alongside quill pens, ballpoints, grease pencils, charcoal markers, and crayons. Seen in this light, the Paintstik is both progressive (more humane than the branding iron) and retro (in our keyboard-driven age, here's a product you actually *handwrite* with), which is a nice combination.

La-Co Industries, Inc.

All of which may be fine and good, but what does the Paintstik offer to those of us who aren't livestock farmers? I tried using it to write my initials on my cats (just picture the "Lost Pet" flier I'd be able to distribute if one of them ran away), but they wouldn't sit still long enough for me to

make a good mark and were too furry anyway — I think I'd probably have to shave them first in order to get the proper effect. Humans, on the other hand, aren't very furry at all, especially young humans, which suggests an obvious application for the Paintstik: use it to mark up your kids in case they get separated from you at the supermarket or department store. It's all too easy for a child to get lost in today's hustle-and-bustle world, so using the Paintstik to draw an easily identified symbol on your precious one's forehead could prevent heartache down the road. The Paintstik is nontoxic, and I found that the bright pigment washed off easily when I tried it on my arm, so there's really very little risk involved. Face it, until they get jobs and learn to clean out the garage, children aren't very different from livestock anyway. You may as well treat them accordingly.

FOUR

There's consumption, and then there's consumption. The best stuff to consume is the
stuff we *literally* consume — the stuff we
eat. And nowhere is the engine of consumer productivity busier than in the realm of food, where the corporate desire to cater to (or, better still, shape) our
tastes has resulted in a marketplace full of very interesting products for our eating enjoyment. Of course,
as the following breakdown of foodstuffs suggests,
some of these products are even more interesting
than they were probably meant to be.

I don't know about you, but the mere thought of this product sends the sound of Shirley Temple's prepubescent voice warbling through my brain. Despite this annoyance, Animal Crackers are among the few mass-produced items that *always* deliver the goods, time after time. The pure simplicity of shortbread, the kick of creating animal amputees and decapitees as you eat, the fun of watching vegetarians flinch before they gobble up the zebra — who could ask for more?

The Animal Crackers box is adorned with lots of animals, along with assorted circus imagery. The basic design is a good one, although nobody questions why the giraffe is depicted as being the same size as, say, the kangaroo. While you may intuitively assume that all the boxes are the same, there are in fact three different package designs currently circulating: a yellow box with blue trim, a blue box trimmed in yellow and red, and a red box trimmed in yellow.

Although each box contains cookie versions of the com-

plete Animal Crackers menagerie, each box *design* displays only a small portion of the product line's zoological offerings. And herein lies Animal Crackers' one real flaw: inexcusable animal redundancy. The yellow box, for instance, features a black panther, the blue box a leopard, and the red box a tiger; they look distinct enough on the boxes, but I'm afraid they haven't made the journey from drawing board to cookie with all their distinguishing features intact. Go on, just *try* to tell which is which when you're serving Animal Crackers for dessert at a summer picnic or when you're sitting in a dark bar, washing down your Animal Crackers with a 50-cent short beer. Likewise, I'm sure the decision to include both a coyote (blue box) and a red fox (yellow box) must have seemed a promising way to diversify the Animal Crackers gene pool, but I can't tell one from the other. Likewise for the bison (red box) and the musk ox (blue box).

Such minor quibbles, however, are no match for the one packaging element that sets Animal Crackers head and shoulders above such overrated snack foodstuffs as Cracker Jack and Gummi Bears. I refer, of course, to the very satisfying little string handle attached to each box. The string wasn't included as part of the original Animal Crackers package design when the product was launched in 1902, but was quickly added later that year. According to Nabisco, the idea was to encourage consumers to hang the boxes from their Christmas trees, a marketing pitch that seems a tad far-fetched to me. But no matter—the string is charming to the eye, soft to the touch, and, I'm happy to report, 100-percent cotton. Remove it from the box, tie it into a miniature lasso, and you can even start your own zoo rodeo with your Animal Crackers, which is precisely the sort of interactive product potential so sorely needed in today's stagnant American marketplace.

RESER'S BULL WHIP BEEF PEPPER STIX, 4-OUNCE SIZE

F rankly, I like meat. Preferably *lots* of meat, thank you very much, and ideally lots of heavily spiced meat. Beef jerky, therefore, is among the very real pleasures of my life. I refer here to *real* beef jerky, not those mass-produced Slim Jims. That stuff is a bunch of foul-smelling, nitrite-laden crap.

Forewarned is supposed to be forearmed, but for many years I nonetheless found myself making a ritual trip to the corner deli, where once a year, like clockwork, I would pound my fist on the counter and demand a stick of mass-produced beef jerky. I don't know what possessed me during this period—I think it was that the Slim Jims always *looked* so good, like miniature salamis or bite-sized pepperonis, thereby seducing and overcoming my better judgment. In any event, one bite was always enough to make me wonder what I'd been thinking, until I finally came to my senses and broke out of the one-Slim-Jim-per-annum routine.

I thought I'd conquered this problem once and for all, but the Bull Whip, which I encountered recently at an Arizona truck stop, ups the beef jerky ante considerably. It successfully overwhelms all notions of quality by virtue of sheer quantity: The Bull Whip is *a yard long.* This sort of postbovine extravaganza definitely gets my attention. A quick perusal of the long, floor-mounted display tube that housed a dozen or so Bull Whips revealed a suitably hyperbolic marketing slogan—"Crack the Whip!"—and upon querying the checkout attendant I learned that "everyone loves 'em, the guys eat 'em while they're driving!" Now, I happened to be manning the passenger seat on this journey, but I figured the Bull Whip would taste just as

RESER'S
FINER FOODS

good from that vantage point, so I pulled one out of the tube, returned to the car, and prepared to feast.

After wrestling the thing into a workable eating position —no mean feat when you're dealing with three solid feet of meat detritus—I dug in for that glorious first bite. How I failed to notice the alarm bells sounding in my brain is something that still puzzles me. Suffice it to say that one bite into the Bull Whip's USDA-approved essence was enough to put me off my feed for the next several hours. Another painful lesson learned, and this time let's hope it's for good.

GUYCAN CORNED MUTTON, 12-OUNCE CAN

S ome products manage to combine packaging, contents, and context in a manner that fairly *demands* consumer attention. Such is the case with this Uruguayan canned good, which recently made its debut at my local supermarket. It began casting its spell on me with an excellent retro-styled label design. Upon closer inspection I encountered the basic product name —"Corned Mutton"—and, zooming in closer still, discovered the fine print: "With juices added." By this point I was pretty intrigued. Then I noticed the sheep.

Believe me, Tony the Tiger, Charlie the Tuna, and Morris the Cat have nothing on the Guycan sheep. He stands there on the

BEDESSEE
IMPORTS, INC.

label, silhouetted on a plain white background, staring directly at you and, I swear, pouting. His posture and demeanor suggest one simple message: "Go on, buy the fucking thing." By now I didn't need much persuasion, but then Guycan delivered their knockout punch—the ingredients listing. First ingredient: "Cooked mutton." Second ingredient: "Mutton." Ah yes, I do like a product that has all the bases covered, muttonwise. Throw all these elements together and, as I'm sure you'll agree, you're bound to make pretty potent inroads into many a wallet. Now imagine a *three-foot-high display rack* of this product and you'll see that my $1.89 and I never stood a chance.

Cooler than Spam, more grammatical than Treet, and easier to say three times fast than Hormel Potted Meat Food Product, Corned Mutton shows all the signs of becoming the next big white-trash lunch bonanza. And how does it taste, you ask? Don't ask.

SALAMIDA'S ORIGINAL STATE FAIR SPIEDIE SAUCE MARINADE, 16-OUNCE BOTTLE

I n the 1978 version of *Invasion of the Body Snatchers*, there's a scene where Leonard Nimoy (still typecast as an alien, even without the ears) explains how he and his fellow pod-people drift through space until they find suitable planets to infiltrate. "We adapt, and we survive," he says. "The function of life *is* survival."

Well, that's all very nice, but it's bullshit. The Function of Life is to eat spiedies, period. The tragedy is that unless you've spent some time living in the upstate New York town of Binghamton, you have no idea what I'm talking about and are consequently out of luck. So listen up: Spiedies (say, "SPEE-deez") are cubes of pork, veal, lamb, beef, or chicken (roadkill will do in a pinch) marinated in this incredible sauce that sort of resembles Italian dressing but definitely goes beyond the realm of the ordinary. After soaking for a few days, the meat is skewered and BBQ'd, although in cold-weather months I've found the broiler to be an acceptable vehicle as well. The cooked meat, still on the skewer, is served with a piece of super-squishy Italian bread, which is used like a mitt to remove the meat from the stick, a process that creates a sort of mini-sandwich. Dig in.

Different venues have their own variations on the spiedie sauce formula. If you're ever in Binghamton, the acknowledged king of the hill is Sharkey's, on Glenwood just past the intersection of Clinton, where they let the spiedies soak in big galvanized trash cans for a week or so before bringing them up to the kitchen. A good backup is Zopp's, corner of Henry and Liberty, where they'll serve you an insane amount of spiedies on a hard roll. The truly intrepid might want to venture Binghamton-ward for the first weekend in August, when they hold the annual SpiedieFest—just remember to fast for about a week in advance.

Since I suspect very few of you will bother to trek to Bingoland, here's a shortcut: Get on the phone and score yourself a case or so of Salamida's Sauce. Rob Salamida went to court to get exclusive commercial rights to the "Original State Fair" wording in his product name, and once you taste something that's soaked in his sauce for a few days, you'll be offering to help pay off his legal fees.

The next time you find a worm wriggling around in your apple (or, as I recently experienced, in your Mr. Goodbar), comfort yourself with the thought that the folks at Hotlix have been peddling FDA-approved worms for several years now. Grab yourself a tequila- or apple-flavored Hotlix lollipop and sure enough, there's a genuine worm in there, frozen into place and clearly visible inside the transparent lolly like a fly in amber.

Apparently a big deal for some time now in the West — I've found them to be as ubiquitous as Snickers in the truck stops and 7-Elevens of Arizona — Hotlix are a bit harder to come by east of the Mississippi. Not that easterners are missing out on much in the way of a credible edible — the lollies smell like Lysol, taste like Windex, and have that singularly synthetic aftertaste so common in sugar-free foods. And that's *before* you get to the worm. But it's all worth it just for the straight-faced ingredients listing: "Hydrogenated starch hydrolysate, insect larva, natural or artificial flavoring and coloring."

The more detail-oriented among you should now be jumping up and down, yelling, "Wait a minute, worms aren't insects!" True enough. And the sad fact of the matter is that worms just aren't cut out to be baked into the center of a lollipop either. Not that the Hotlix folks didn't try, of course — one variety of worm they tested turned unappetizingly black when cooked; another literally exploded; another shrank; several others failed the taste test.

And so the Hotlix honchos, driven by the true entrepreneurial spirit that fuels only the greatest merchandising endeavors, chose the larval form of the *tenebrio molitor* beetle for their lollipop. They used to raise the li'l critters themselves, fattening 'em up on a diet of cornmeal, apples, and carrots, but business got so good that Hotlix's in-house beetle-birthing operation was stretched beyond capacity. Additional beetles are now shipped in to meet the demand.

$$ Lollipop

The gross fascination some of you are no doubt experiencing at this moment is to be expected—Hotlix tend to provoke a reaction along the lines of "That's really gross! Uh, lemme have one." Want to get in on the fun? Call 1-800-EAT-WORM.

HOSTESS CUP CAKES WITH CREAMY FILLING, 3.2-OUNCE PACK

I've always loved this product. Twenty years ago, I used my milk money to buy Hostess Cup Cakes; these days, they're an indispensable ingredient in my favorite dessert, Junk Food à la Mode. And they're still a good choice for the occasional snack on my way to or from the subway.

That said, I've got a bone to pick with the folks at Hostess. The spongy cake, the endearingly synthetic frosting, and the injection-pumped filling are fine, and the ingredients listing still functions nicely as a junior-college chemistry lesson, but my favorite part of eating Hostess Cup Cakes was always removing the cakes from the cardboard base on which they sat and then running my finger along the piece of cardboard, thereby salvaging the pastry residue that inevitably stuck there. An informal poll of acquaintances reveals that I am far from the only cupcake consumer to have savored the joys of the finger swipe, a consideration that apparently eluded the folks at Hostess a

few years back when they replaced the cardboard base with an unsatisfying premolded plastic tray.

It's worth noting here that most other Hostess products, from the timeless Twinkies to the noxious yet oddly compelling Suzy Q's, remain packaged on the familiar piece of cardboard. So why the cupcake switcheroo? A call to the Hostess Consumer Affairs line reveals that the reason was "damage control — the cupcakes kept getting squashed by improper handling and rough treatment during shipping." Nobody could explain to me why the other Hostess goodies, which boast similar squishiness factors, haven't suffered from this problem.

CONTINENTAL
BAKING COMPANY

My advice to those of you who think Twinkie residue is finger-lickin' good is to get it while you still can.

HOSTESS TWINKIES, 2.7-OUNCE PACK

My ire aroused by the cavalier packaging treatment afforded Hostess Cup Cakes (see above), I found myself gravitating more toward Twinkies. But no sooner had I switched allegiances than a new Hostess issue emerged.

One of my favorite things about Hostess Twinkies (and Cup Cakes and Suzy Q's, for that matter) is the subtle granular quality to the creamy filling. If you've ever eaten a Hostess product, you probably know what I'm talking about—there's an ever-so-slight grittiness to the filling, a grainy toothiness that's most evident when you "chew" some of the filling between your molars. I've always attributed this to confectioner's sugar that failed to dissolve completely, although some friends have long maintained that it's due to the presence of suet (the ingredients listing does include "beef fat," so I suppose they could be right). Anyway, whatever its source, this inconspicuous textural quality has become an important part of my Twinkie experience.

So important, in fact, that when I was in Chicago recently and bought some Twinkies with smooth, decidedly nongranular filling, I assumed I'd purchased a defective pack. So I brought them back to the store and exchanged them, only to be disappointed once again. Then I walked down the street and bought a pack at another store —still no grittiness. Intrigued (okay, obsessed) by this development, I spent the next several days sampling Twinkies all over Chi-town. By week's end

I'd concluded that *Chicago Twinkies simply don't have faintly granular filling like New York Twinkies.*

And neither, I soon discovered, do San Francisco Twinkies, Austin Twinkies, Toledo Twinkies, Indianapolis Twinkies, Columbus Twinkies, or Reno Twinkies. I had first assumed that the Chicago confections were some sort of aberration, but now I was beginning to wonder if my beloved graininess might actually be the *exception,* not the rule. Upset by the implications of these regional variations, and figuring the Hostess honchos would share my concern, I mailed off an inquiry to their consumer affairs department.

Within a week I had my reply. "The filling is a standard formula," explained the very unsatisfying letter from Hostess, "with slight variations to compensate for altitude, water, and different suppliers of ingredients in [our 30] bakeries. . . . Steps have already been taken to alert the General Manager of our bakery so that he may be aware also." Yeah, right. Fortunately, the same reflexive twitch that led Hostess to send me this form letter also led them to enclose a complimentary coupon good for a free package of Hostess products, up to a $3 value. By happy coincidence, I know exactly where my supermarket shelves the Twinkie 10-packs, and I think they cost $2.99.

BLIND ROBINS SMOKED OCEAN HERRING, 0.25-OUNCE SIZE

've downed many a beer in many a bar, and I thought I'd seen everything when it came to bar food, from cherry bombs to pickled eggs. But a recent impromptu visit to Snyder's Tavern, a comfortable little dive on Route 28A in the Catskills, revealed that I hadn't seen jack.

Snyder's features a wide array of charms for seducing the road-weary traveler, including a great exterior sign, a 50-cent pool table, a congenial bartender named Norm, a bunch of gorgeous old photographs, a taxidermed bobcat, and a generally friendly crowd ranging from hunters and fishermen to hunter-gatherers. I was in the middle of my second Budweiser, taking it all in, when I noticed a display rack of cellophane-wrapped snacks at the far end of the bar. There was a lot of glare coming off the plastic, so I couldn't be sure I was reading the packages properly, but they appeared to say, "Blind Robins Smoked Ocean Herring." This was uncharted territory — I had to know more.

I asked Norm for a pack of the stuff. The sliced strips of herring, visible through the clear package, looked like giant slugs — none too appetizing. "Do you sell many of these?" I

Bar Food
Products

INTERLUDE: A VISIT TO THE SUPERMARKET

New York is a great city and all, but one of the worst things about living here is the utter dearth of adequate supermarkets. I know, I know — space is at a premium and square footage is expensive, but that doesn't make the situation any less of a drag. To the avid product aesthete, the supermarket is, well, a *super market.* It's more than just a place to pick up milk and eggs — it's a testament to what's left of America's producer economy, a place to savor the unique stimulatory rush provided by an ocean of products, a rush that mere services can never hope to match. For sheer consumer overload, only the hardware store and the office-supply outlet can rival the supermarket, but they both cater to specialists. The supermarket remains one of our culture's most inspired forums because it caters (okay, panders) to *everyone.*

Like most people, I have a basic series of staples that I buy just about every time I hit the supermarket, and I ➡➡

asked Norm. "Tons," he replied, conjuring up unpleasant images of bulldozed mountains of herring in my mind. "They're really salty," added the gent to my left. "You break off a slice and put it between your lip and gum. It reminds you to keep drinking."

Thanks, but I don't need to be reminded. Fortunately, this product doesn't have to be consumed to be enjoyed. As is so often the case, the real pleasure lies in the package design. Or, more specifically, in the Blind Robins logo, a beautifully simple two-color illustration of a red-breasted bird with a handkerchief tied around its face. So "Blind Robins" turns out to be a brilliant misnomer—this bird isn't blind, he's blind*folded*. It's not clear if the manufacturer is suggesting that the blindfold is a recommended accessory when eating smoked ocean herring, but I say anyone downing this stuff shouldn't stop there—throw in a cigarette and a firing squad and get it over with.

usually bring along a shopping list of additional items. But I also try to keep my eyes open for interesting products that I don't really want or need, things that strike me as intriguing, entertaining, puzzling, or some combination thereof. And in a commercial landscape filled with familiar brand names and logos that we've seen again and again for decades, I try to stay alert for consumer revelations and epiphanies that I might have overlooked or previously taken for granted.

In New York, however, this is harder than it sounds. Shelf space is limited, brand choice is consequently restricted, and lots of new products never even make it here. The severity of the situation was driven home during a recent road trip, when I happened to stop in at a classic suburban supermarket. I was greeted by an immense floor-to-ceiling display featuring scores of products, aptly named the "Wall of Savings." As I stared at this monument to retailing abundance, I realized just what I'd been missing in New York. Fuck the savings, man—I just want the wall.

MEETER'S KRAUT JUICE, 10-OUNCE CAN
FRANK'S QUALITY KRAUT JUICE, 18-OUNCE THREE-PACK
SILVER FLOSS BARREL-CURED KRAUT JUICE, 22-OUNCE FOUR-PACK
S&W SAUERKRAUT JUICE, 10-OUNCE CAN

T he concept of inconspicuous consumption is a sophisticated one, but that's not to suggest that it's completely immune to the forces of destiny, serendipity, or popular demand. These are precisely the elements that converged upon me during a recent 17-day period, when three separate out-of-town acquaintances, ranging from two

While my local Brooklyn supermarket is no match for such muscular displays of grocery-driven might, it is nonetheless capable of providing me with some interesting shopping. Our first stop is the cereal aisle, which, as I learned back in college, is one of the most dynamic spots in any supermarket. In those undergraduate days I worked a twice-weekly graveyard proofreading shift on my school paper, where we'd usually break at about three in the morning for a food run that routinely featured cold cuts, chips, and cereal. Our goal was to never buy the same cereal twice, which turned out to be surprisingly easy—really big supermarkets carry all sorts of short-lived cereals you've never heard of, many of them resulting from misguided licensing deals designed to cash in on this TV show or that movie or whatever. Had you worked on my school paper, you too might have eaten Mr. T Cereal.

The latest offering to catch my eye in this aisle is Reese's Peanut Butter Puffs (General Mills), the sort ➡➡

casual pals who barely know me at all to an ex-girlfriend who knows me as well as anyone, rang me up and said, "I've got just the product for you, you're gonna love this: kraut juice." As in *sauer*kraut juice. As in the juice of fermented cabbage. Um, is someone trying to tell me something?

After arranging to have my colleagues ship me the goods, I found myself plunged into the briny and surprisingly varied depths of kraut juice. My journey turned out to be typically obsessive, but in this case my single-mindedness was understandable. For starters, I'd never heard of kraut juice before and couldn't find it at any of my local supermarkets. A certain doggedness of pursuit was therefore necessary. Moreover, as mass-produced foodstuffs go, I find this one's mere existence to be a tremendous novelty. I mean, come on —*kraut juice?* Get real. When confronted with a product like this one, it's not enough just to bask in its presence; I need to *immerse* myself.

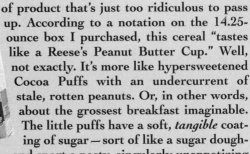

of product that's just too ridiculous to pass up. According to a notation on the 14.25-ounce box I purchased, this cereal "tastes like a Reese's Peanut Butter Cup." Well, not exactly. It's more like hypersweetened Cocoa Puffs with an undercurrent of stale, rotten peanuts. Or, in other words, about the grossest breakfast imaginable. The little puffs have a soft, *tangible* coating of sugar — sort of like a sugar doughnut — and sport a pasty, singularly unappetizing color that makes them look like they're halfway down the road to Rancid City. You can bet that it's going to take more than the old advertising line about "two great tastes that taste great together" to effectively promote this stuff. I'm not throwing my box away, though — I have a feeling it may come in handy one day as a hangover cure.

A solid aisle or two of canned goods forms the backbone of any good supermarket, and it's here that things start get-

We should begin with the name. Although the colloquialism *kraut juice*—as opposed to the more formal *sauerkraut juice*—confusingly suggests the image of a German being squeezed on a rack, I've nonetheless concluded that the shorter, more conversational term is important, as three of the four brands that were forwarded to me use it as their official product name, chopping the lengthier word down to size without so much as an apostrophe. None of my associates could give me any historical background on this etymological foreshortening, but on one thing they could agree: by any name, the stuff is rank.

I can readily add my own voice to this chorus of derision. Kraut juice deserves its own wing in the gustatory hall of shame, and I say that without even having tasted the stuff. Not that I didn't try, mind you—KJ smells like a cross between a malfunctioning septic tank and a poorly ventilated poultry farm, and one quick whiff was enough to kick my

ting interesting. Thanks to the twin miracles of vacuum packing and nitrite preservatives, our nation's foodstuff purveyors have figured out how to put just about any meat-related substance in a can. Chipped beef, Vienna sausages, Spam, hash, something called "luncheon meat with natural juices"—you name it, they've found a way to process it into something that looks just like cat food.

My interest this day focuses on the surprisingly large variety of canned seafood. The obvious tuna, sardines, and anchovies notwithstanding, my supermarket offers a fair amount of canned seagoing fare from which to choose: clams, herring, scungilli, several types of salmon (pink, red, medium-red, and blueback), crabmeat, oysters, and mackerel. None of this is packaged with any sort of gourmet or upscale appeal, so the implicit pitch is rather straightforward: save yourself a trip to the fish store and buy our canned stuff instead.

I'm pondering all of this when my gaze settles on a 4.25-ounce can of Marvelous Large Shrimp (Reuther's ➡

gag reflex into overdrive and send me sprinting to open a window. In that respect, at least, I guess we could say that kraut juice is definitely a summer drink.

So if the stuff is so oddball, so hard to come by, and so vile, why are there so many different brands? What accounts for the apparently brisk competition in the kraut juice market? Or, perhaps more to the point, why is there a kraut juice market in the first place?

The superficial aspects of the product itself certainly offer few answers. KJ is a cloudy, vaguely brownish-green liquid, and none of the brands at my disposal showed any differentiation in this regard. An examination of the packaging, however, revealed varied and interesting distinctions. The breakdown, by brand, is as follows:

STOKELY USA, INC.

Seafood Company, Inc.). I love shrimp in just about any form imaginable, so I figure this is a safe purchase. And besides, contrary to what most people think, most of the "fresh" shrimp we buy at the fish store has been frozen into large blocks on its way up from the Gulf of Mexico or South America or wherever. So why not canned shrimp?

Well, for starters, these are the sorriest looking shrimp I've ever seen. They look deformed, contorted, tumorous. They're also structurally suspect—most of them fall to pieces as I pick them out of the can, and the few that survive that ordeal fall apart when I follow the label's instructions to rinse them in cold water before serving. As for taste, let's just say that anyone on a low-sodium diet should stay far, far away.

Then there's the whole issue of size. "Large shrimp" is one of those classic contradictions, of course, but the term achieves new oxymoronic resonance when you open a can of Marvelous shrimp. The little fuckers are practically submicroscopic. I wonder how someone's supposed to eat the

* *Meeter's:* A plain can with a wraparound label glued on, rather than a preprinted can — nice . . . Excellent label design: attractive color palette, pleasing typography, and a good illustration of a friendly-looking glass of KJ, complete with a few frothy bubbles on the surface . . . Manufactured in Oconomowoc, Wisconsin, a town that surely breaks the record for most nonconsecutive uses of the letter *o* . . . Meeter's has thoughtfully provided three "suggested cocktail recipes" for their KJ; unfortunately, these turn out to be nonalcoholic and wildly unimaginative ("Sauerkraut Juice with Lemon: Add 1 tablespoon lemon juice to 1 cup chilled kraut juice").

* *Silver Floss:* A four-pack held together by one of those flexible plastic ring thingies . . . The preprinted cans feature a cheesy, fake-wood-grain background,

"medium" and "small" varieties — with a straw? This aisle has worn out its welcome — let's move on.

Ah, the unfettered beauty of a well-stocked snack food aisle, an enduring and endearing monument to high sodium and raging cholesterol. Will it be potato chips or pretzels? Nachos or mixed nuts? My mind swims with possibilities until my eyes come to rest on a canister of Pringles Original Potato Crisps (Procter & Gamble). Although I haven't tasted Pringles in a good 20 years or so, they happen to have been on my mind lately, thanks to a pen pal who recently cited them as her favorite junk food. "It's the packaging, totally," she explained. "The cool cylinder with the pop-top, so perfectly encasing ➡

presumably to evoke the product's "barrel-cured" properties . . . Boring type treatment, boring illustration . . . At 5.5 ounces per can, this brand offers the smallest ration of KJ — probably a good thing.

✳ *S&W:* Plain can with wraparound label . . . The only brand to employ photography rather than illustration . . . Dreadful typography . . . The only brand to use the lengthier "sauerkraut juice" designation . . . At 10 ounces, tied with Meeter's for the heftiest KJ serving.

✳ *Frank's:* A three-pack, with the individual cans nestled inside a cardboard sleeve . . . Clearly the cream of the kraut juice crop, at least in terms of package design. While all the other brands feature four-color print jobs, Frank's kicks their collective butt while providing a case study in the effective use of two-color design. The individual preprinted cans feature

dozens of IDENTICAL chips — it always reminded me of a time capsule."

This commentary is interesting, because I've always thought of Pringles as a *conceptual* time capsule. They seemed ingeniously, almost prototypically representative of the 1970s when first launched upon an unsuspecting snack food market in the early part of that decade — synthetic, redundant, ultraprocessed, characterless. Who would have guessed they'd still be rolling along at this late date?

My first Pringles purchase in nearly 20 years reveals that this product has undergone virtually no discernible alterations. The saddle-shaped chips (made from a mixture of potato flour and water, not from actual potatoes) are just as vaguely unsatisfying as I remembered — not quite potatoey enough, not quite salty enough, with none of the burnt edges that I love. One thing has changed, however: in 1991 the product was officially renamed, thenceforth to be known as potato *crisps,* rather than *chips.* According to splendid type and a well-rendered illustration of a head of cabbage and a glass of KJ sitting side by side, looking all buddy-buddy — appealing or appalling, depending on my mood . . . The fine print is a riot, serving up a bonanza of unnecessary quotation marks. Frank's, it says here, "is 'deliciously different' . . . with a distinctive 'personality' . . . but [it's] also 'just naturally' GOOD." Plus it "helps you perk up and combat that logy feeling after overindulging" . . . Since the sleeve has its own bar code, the cans themselves are code-free, a huge visual advantage on a small container.

This analysis still left the major KJ questions unanswered. The Meeter's cocktail recipes, however, intrigued me. True, they were boring, but perhaps they hinted at KJ's larger potential as a mixer. My interest piqued, I called my friend Tom, a man who knows a thing or two about mixing a mean

Procter & Gamble spokesperson Judy Ellis, this nomenclatorial alteration was made "because Pringles are not just your ordinary, garden-variety potato chips." As Ellis put it, "Chips break; crisps don't. Chips get stale; crisps stay crisp."

Yeah, and cheese eventually spoils, while Cheez Whiz stays edible forever, but that's not necessarily an improvement. As you might expect, Ellis didn't exactly see it that way, but she did address another question I had: with the advent of 1970s nostalgia, are Pringles suddenly fashionable, and has this been reflected in the product's sales figures? The answer appears to be yes. Ellis reported that Pringles' business has been booming since the early nineties, and while she couldn't be certain how much of this is attributable to the retro factor, she agreed that the resurgence of seventies icons can only be Pringles-positive.

The home-cleanup aisle doesn't deal with foodstuffs, of course, but we may as well deal with it here. This aisle has always bored the hell out of me. Domestic chores are ➧➧

cocktail. And kraut juice, he reported, makes a cocktail that's meaner than most.

"We've tried to make a decent drink using that stuff," he said. "We came up with a few mixtures, gave them names like the Limping Veteran and the Strikebreaker—you know, like, 'Bartender, a Limping Veteran, please, and make it strong!'—but they were all really disgusting. Then we made the mistake of leaving an open can of the stuff in the fridge, and it stank up the whole place. It just reeks."

With kraut juice steadfastly refusing to exhibit any redeeming features other than sheer entertainment value, I had little choice but to contact the manufacturers directly. To my surprise, they were as mystified by KJ as I was.

"I really can't understand how people drink it," said John Gauthier, head of the

annoying enough without having to shell out cash along the way. I resent even having to buy sponges, dishwashing liquid, laundry detergent, scouring powder, Brillo, brooms, mops, and the like. There's virtually no consumer satisfaction in purchasing these ho-hum products, and in a truly enlightened society they would just be provided for us by the state.

What a surprise, then, to find entertainment value lurking in this sector of the supermarket. I refer here to Home Care Disposable Vacuum Cleaner Bags, Styles S & M (Home Care Industries, Inc.), a product whose "S&M" designation cannot be written off as an innocent coincidence. Even if you can accept the notion that vacuum styles "S" and "M" just happen to be functionally equivalent, the basic rules of alphabetization would seem to mitigate against presenting the letters in this sequence on the product's packaging. Perhaps those jokers at Home Care Industries are just trying to see who's paying attention.

As I arrive at the unfortunate retailing ghetto known as

marketing-relations firm that handles Frank's. "I tried a can once, about ten years ago; all my hair turned gray."

You'd expect at least a few of the manufacturers to stick up for their own product, but the other KJ representatives I spoke with essentially echoed

COMSTOCK FOODS

Gauthier. "It's not good-tasting at all," admitted Dick Fink, vice president of marketing for S&W. And when I asked Ken Murray, vice president of sales and marketing for Stokely USA, which produces Meeter's, if he'd ever downed a can of KJ, he replied, "No. I don't have the guts."

So who's buying the stuff? Primarily senior citizens and retirees, my contacts agreed. "The kraut juice business goes way back," said Murray, "and the consumer tends to be older." And just what is this typical consumer seeking when he or she reaches for a can of KJ?

the ethnic aisle, I realize I could use some superhot vinegar, so I check out the assorted brands of vinegar-soaked tabasco peppers, ultimately choosing a bottle of Goya Pickled Peppers (Goya Foods, Inc.). The lid to the Goya bottle, like the lids used by all the other brands, features one of those little nibs that the customer can snip off, thereby transforming the bottle of peppers into a vinegar shaker. I'm admiring this packaging coup when I'm suddenly hit with a revelation: this product is officially listed and described as one thing (peppers), but it's designed to be used as another (vinegar), *and there's absolutely no explicit acknowledgment of this duality.*

If this doesn't sound earthshaking to you, go ahead and name me another grocery item with a comparable personality crisis. And wouldn't you expect Goya to try to take advantage of this product's twofold utility? It seems preposterous that the Goya label doesn't even mention the nib on the bottle lid, and they're totally blowing the chance to say something like, "Also makes a great vinegar shaker ➡➡

"It cleans 'em out and gets 'em running regular," said Gauthier. Murray was more succinct: "It's a *terrific* natural laxative." I found it interesting that this claim was absent from the package designs, but I wasn't about to quibble. At last—an identifiable kraut juice virtue, even if the cure seemed worse than the disease.

As it turns out, KJ lore is rich with purported curative qualities, although the industry folk cautioned that most were probably apocryphal. "I have letters," said Janice Price, marketing director for Comstock Foods, which handles Silver Floss. "People have written in and said that sauerkraut juice has saved them from their deathbeds." In a somewhat less dramatic claim, Fink said some of his customers soaked their feet in KJ to combat athlete's foot.

KJ's utility in other areas appears to be limited. Although it's marketed as a drink, nobody I spoke with really believed

to spice up your foods!" Apparently they just assume that you'll know what to do. I became so obsessed with this missed marketing opportunity that I actually called Goya, where Marketing Director Conrad Colon stammered some lame excuse about not having enough space on the label (a false claim, as this photo shows).

As I swing my cart around toward the checkout counter, I pass a display rack of one of my favorite recent products: Gulden's Spicy Brown Mustard Packets To-Go (American Home Food Products, Inc.), a box of 30 small packets of Gulden's mustard. It takes one snazzy packaging job—not to mention a fair amount of chutzpah—to make me buy a product that I could easily get for free at McDonald's or from the hot dog vendor at the ballpark, but the Gulden's folks have outdone themselves with the Gulden's To-Go box. The that anyone would drink it without an ulterior medicinal motive ("Oh, I assume there's *someone* out there who likes it—there must be," said Fink). And what about culinary applications? Measuring his words carefully, Gauthier said, "Now, I have no scientific proof of this, but it seems to have a tenderizing effect on meat when used as a marinade." I told him I'd take his word for it.

As for the cocktail angle, there was general agreement that your local bar need not stock KJ, although, on the other side of the alcoholic equation, Gauthier was aware of a drink called the Ting Tang, a 1:1 mixture of KJ and tomato juice that he said works well as a hangover cure. "Back in the forties they put it in cans and sold the hell out of it," he said, adding that the president of the Fremont Company, which distributes Frank's, is in the annual habit of declaring his

magnificent five-color design, neither retro nor postmodern, is brilliantly executed in every detail, from the color scheme and the dynamite pair of illustrations to the typography and the background detailing. And unlike most sophisticated package designs, this one isn't selling a lifestyle; it's just selling mustard. And it has sold some to me.

I'll probably never use the annoying little mustard packets, of course, but it doesn't matter. Consumer satisfaction is where you find it, and on this shopping trip I have found it several times over on the conceptual level. I head for the checkout line, secure in the knowledge that on this day at least, the supermarket has lived up to its name.

intention to bring Ting Tang back to the market, a promise (or threat) on which he has yet to make good.

And what does the future hold for KJ? The consensus was that the market trend is definitely down. This assessment was seconded by Richard Hentschel, executive vice president of the National Kraut Packers Association, who told me, "It's just one of those unfortunate products that has fallen by the wayside."

Well, not completely. Gauthier, who, like the others, said his brand has been around at least since the Depression, pointed out that KJ's audience is "very small but very loyal." Indeed, despite all the ridicule, my contacts alerted me to the existence of at least four additional brands (the most prominent of which appears to be Flannagan's, manufactured by what Murray termed "big honchos in the Wisconsin kraut business"). And Hentschel, while unable to quote precise figures, gave me enough raw data to figure out that a good 100,000 gallons of KJ are sloshing around out there each year. A frightening thought, to be sure.

BACON CURLS ORIGINAL FLAVOR MICROWAVE PORK RINDS, 1.75-OUNCE BAG

I t's not clear whether Bacon Curls Microwave Pork Rinds have been harvested from Pig Improvement Company porkers (see Chapter 6), but one thing is certain: it's worth owning a microwave just to have an excuse to buy this product.

Bacon Curls rinds, packaged in a bag just like the ones used for microwave popcorn, offer an interactive snacking experience that's pretty tough to beat. As the product name suggests, the rinds start out as small pork snippets that look very much like bacon scraps. Nuke the little guys for three or four minutes, however, and they pop, sizzle, contort, and expand to become full-fledged pork rinds, just like the ones that nobody buys down at the corner deli. There's no explanation as to precisely what sort of alchemy is responsible for this metamorphosis, and maybe that's just as well—knowing the secret might ruin the fun.

Pork rinds aren't anyone's idea of health food, but I suppose nothing should surprise me in a market where Domino Sugar touts itself as a low-calorie food product. So if the folks behind Bacon Curls want to pretend that their pork rinds belong on the cover of *Prevention* magazine, who am I to scoff? "60% Less Fat Than Fried Pork Rinds!" trumpets the packaging in three different spots, with some additional fine print thrown in about protein value. Hey, guys, while you're at it, why not point out that the rinds are also sugar-, caffeine-, and preservative-free?

CURTICE
BURNS MEAT
SNACKS, INC.

Most of the rest of the package is devoted to microwaving directions and some very weak ad copy: "You'll hear them sizzlin' all the way to your bowl!" Having tried a bag of these things, however, I must report that this is either a typo or an understatement; you'll actually hear them sizzling all the way to your *bowel.*

MISTER SALTY PRETZEL TWISTS, 9-OUNCE BOX

ontemporary trends in healthful eating aren't just an inconvenience—they've also resulted in perfectly functional brand names like Kentucky Fried Chicken and Sugar Crisp devolving into obfuscatory gibberish like KFC and Golden Crisp (very confusing for

those of us who believe you are what you eat). With this in mind, let's take a few moments to salute Mister Salty, a brand name that proudly continues to fly its banner of high-sodium indulgence.

Of course, the real reason for Mister Salty's longevity may be that no substitute name is readily apparent. What would the options be — Mister Sodium Chloride? Mister Little White Flavor Crystals? Mister Hypertension? Mister Fluid Retention?

As it turns out, neither these choices nor any others have been considered. That news comes from Nabisco spokesperson Ann Smith, who explained, "Mister Salty is over thirty years old and has strong brand recognition. We wouldn't want to change that."

Point well taken. But it seems to me that the Mister Salty moniker also presents some limitations. At a time when many pretzel manufacturers are offering low-salt and salt-free versions of their products, for example, Nabisco's hands would appear to be tied. You don't have to be a marketing whiz to deduce that Salt-Free Mister Salty is not going to fly off the shelves.

Not to worry, according to Smith. "Nabisco has products that run the gamut of tastes," she happily informed me. "We make products for everyone. For consumers who want a high-quality baked product with a nice salty flavor, Mister Salty fills a niche."

Fine, but given the health-conscious scent in the wind, is it a *diminishing* niche? Apparently not, says Smith. "We've never had any feedback from consumers who wanted a low-sodium variety. And anyway," she added, getting rather disingenuous even by PR standards at this point,

NABISCO
FOODS, INC.

"nutritionists will tell you that you need a certain amount of salt in your diet." Ah yes, Mister Salty, guardian of the public health. For those incorrigibles who insist on flouting this sage medical guidance, Smith recommended Nabisco's Mr. Phipps Pretzel Chips, which come in a low-sodium variety.

In any event, said Smith, sodium is yesterday's news. Today's food paranoia centers on fat, and pretzels are a low-fat snack. Consumers, egged on by marketing campaigns, began figuring this out a few years ago, leading to increased pretzel sales for most brands, Mister Salty included.

As for Mister Salty himself, still smiling that big white grin after more than three decades on the job, he appears to be something of a mystery man. "No one knows exactly where he came from or who created him," said Smith. "Basically, he's always stood for the quality of the brand."

Which brings up a pet peeve of mine. The Mister Salty box describes the product as "pretzel *twists*"—in other words, the familiar Dutch pretzel shape. But these pretzels, like so many now on the market, no longer fit this description. The two looping arcs on each side of the pretzel swing around and meet in the center, but they do *not* twist around each other like the pretzels of yore. If Mister Salty really wants to stand behind his product, he'd better wipe that grin off his face and start working on some quality control, pronto.

LIFE SAVERS CANDIES, MUSK AND THIRST FLAVORS, 20-GRAM ROLLS

According to *Webster's*, musk is either a scent gland or just a scent, but try telling that to the folks at Nestlé Confectioners. They think musk is a flavor, and I've got the roll of Life Savers to prove it.

No, you can't just run down to the corner store and grab your own roll. And no, you haven't been overlooking something at the candy rack for all these years. These Life Savers hail from Australia, where my friend Barb discovered them at a gas station during a recent trip Down Under.

Rest assured, however, that while musk-flavored Life Savers come from another hemisphere, they're still very much the real thing. The wrapper sports the familiar Life Savers logo, as well as the somewhat annoying "Get a Hole Lot More Out of Life" slogan (which has thankfully fallen into disuse here in the States, where the wrappers simply say, "The candy with the hole"). The candies themselves have the words "Life Savers" stamped into them, just like their American counterparts.

So let's say you were working for a company that decided to market a musk-flavored snack — what color would you choose for the packaging? And what color would you use for the product itself? Well, if you were working for Nestlé Confectioners in Australia, you'd choose pink for the background of the wrapper, with big red lettering for the word "Musk." You'd also choose a sort of frosted pink for the candies. And what would your food chemists use to approximate the taste of something that isn't a taste? Thanks to the apparent laxity of Australian product-labeling laws, we'll probably never know, because there's no ingredients listing on the wrapper.

And maybe that's just as well. Whatever they put in there, it makes for a very odd snacking experience. The initial sensation is extremely sweet, but this soon gives way to something much harder to describe, something sort of like . . . raw meat. Or, as the guy who sold them to Barb put it, "They're sort of an acquired taste." I suppose none of this should surprise me, coming as it does from a country where everyone happily consumes Vegemite. In fact, I'd barely come to terms with the whole Musk phenomenon when my Australian friend David told me of another interesting Life Saver flavor they have down there: *Thirst*.

Thirst Life Savers, like their musk-flavored cousins, present something of a puzzle. Whereas Musk turns reason on its head by making a flavor out of something more commonly known as a scent, Thirst takes things a step further by making a flavor *out of an abstract condition*. Taken to its logical extreme, this approach suggests a whole series of like-minded flavors — Hunger, Restlessness, Arousal, Satisfaction, Drowsiness, Pain, Indifference, and so on. There's also this question to ponder: Do they quench your thirst, or do they make you thirsty?

After a quick taste test, I can report that my immediate instinct upon trying one was to reach for a glass of water, although this had more to do with the intense desire to rinse out my mouth than with genuine thirst per se. Thirst Life Savers have a singularly awful flavor — I'd like to describe it as "dried pee and blood plasma," but it turns out that the author of this book's foreword already did that several years ago. Instead, I'll go with the following: powdered Gatorade mixed with a raw-egg coagulant. Are you getting the idea?

NESTLÉ CONFECTIONERS, LTD.

Such critiques notwithstanding, David says Musk and Thirst are two of the more popular Life Savers flavors Down Under. "I went through a bit of a Thirst phase as a youth myself," he says, appearing none the worse for wear from the experience. Fine, fine — to each his own and all that. But I'll be sticking with Wild Cherry for the foreseeable future.

PILOT'S BEER, 17-OUNCE BOTTLE • • • • • • • • • • • • • • • • • • •

The year 1997 marks the 60th anniversary of the *Hindenburg* disaster. We've all seen the photos of the 803-foot airship bursting into flames as it approached its moorings in Lakehurst, New Jersey. We've all heard the tape of the live radio feed, with the announcer bawling, "Oh, the humanity . . ." We all know a bunch of people died —three dozen, to be exact—when the craft's hydrogen bays ignited.

What nobody knows, even after six decades and loads of conspiracy theories, is what caused it all. But I've developed my own hunch on the subject since my friend Matt went to Germany and brought me back a bottle of Pilot's Beer, a medium-dark brew with a remarkable package design. The Pilot's Beer bottle—which is conventionally shaped but made out of reinforced aluminum, not glass—features an illustration of a stately-looking zeppelin cruising grandly among the cumulonimbi. Just above this is a portrait of airship pioneer Ferdinand Graf von Zeppelin himself. The rest of the design is given over to an assortment of copy printed in an array of languages, but you don't have to be multilingual to decipher the implicit message: Pilot's is the one beer to have when you happen to be skippering a dirigible.

I wonder what Mothers Against Drunk Driving would think of Pilot's Beer. They certainly wouldn't be pleased with the extended product line I'm envisioning. Imagine if you will a school bus driver helming a yellow bus full of happy youngsters while sucking down a bottle of Bus Driver's Beer. Or an Amtrak locomotive with a guy getting tipsy on Engineer's Beer at the controls. Or maybe a bottle of Captain's Beer,

MANUFACTURER UNCERTAIN

complete with a portrait of *Exxon Valdez* fall guy Joseph Hazelwood. The DWI possibilities are limited only by the number of transportation modes you can dream up.

Hindenburg pilot Max Pruss was badly burned in the 1937 explosion but was among the survivors. Did anyone think to give him a quick Breathalyzer test? I'm convinced he was the ultimate drunk driver, sloshed out of his skull on Pilot's Beer. Pruss has since died, so any secrets of this sort went with him to the grave. But next time I see a Goodyear blimp floating overhead, I wanna know what those guys are drinking up there.

SWEET ONES DIET DESSERT SPRAYS, ASSORTED FLAVORS

I'm lucky enough to be relatively trim and fit. As we all know, however, the weight-loss industry cynically cultivates and then exploits the negative self-image of millions of less fortunate souls. This practice appears to have reached its apex—or nadir, I guess—with Sweet Ones, a diet product that can best be described as loathsomely amusing.

How loathsome? Sweet Ones are yet another product line trying to peddle the old somethin'-for-nothin' scam that you can have your cake (or, in this case, your banana split, chocolate mousse, peaches 'n' cream, or strawberry shortcake), eat it too, and still not gain weight. And how amusing? So amusing that they purport to achieve this with a *pump spray.* It's a diet-plan version of the Binaca Blast.

I'm a sucker for almost any sort of clever gadget, and so I confess to finding the Sweet Ones canister extremely appealing on a purely mechanical level. At first glance it looks sort of like a mascara applicator: a small metal cylinder, four inches long by five-eighths of an inch wide. Pick a flavor, remove the cap to reveal the pump, position the nozzle in front of your open mouth, and spray away —*bon appétit*.

The idea, of course, is to use Sweet Ones in lieu of a real dessert. "When you get the urge for something sweet and rich, satisfy it with Sweet Ones," says the package. "It only *tastes* fattening."

Actually, it doesn't taste like much of anything, which makes sense —each one-calorie Sweet Ones spritz measures about three-thousandths of a fluid ounce, which means it wouldn't satisfy a gerbil in the midst of a 20-day hunger strike, much less an overweight adult grappling with a raging sweet tooth. Despite this, the official Sweet Ones serving size is listed as one spray, which allows the manufacturer to put a very entertaining chart on the back of the package. Here we learn that a real banana split has 1,400 calories, while a spritz of the corresponding Sweet Ones flavor has . . . *one!* Similarly, a serving of chocolate mousse has 700 calories, while its Sweet Ones counterpart has . . . well, you get the idea.

Sweet Ones were sent my way by my West Coast pen pal Kim. She found them at a local 99-cent store, which, as she puts it, is "the last refuge for failed foodstuffs and gizmos." This turns out to be a remarkably accurate description, at least as it pertains to Sweet Ones: The little canisters are gizmos unto themselves, they

NUTRAMAX PRODUCTS, INC.

deliver a metered dose of an alleged foodstuff, and when I wrote to the manufacturer requesting more information, my letter came back marked, "Moved, left no address." Find 'em if you can.

SLIMCHIPS TORTILLA CHIPS, 0.75-OUNCE BAG

I f Sweet Ones (see above) display an unrivaled level of dietetic chutzpah, then SlimChips, a low-fat tortilla snack, are a close second. In order to play up the low-fat angle, the chips have been given their own slogan: "What less could a body ask for?" This turns out to be a telling query indeed, because you couldn't very well ask for less of this product than they're already offering you—the SlimChips bag is practically empty. *Literally.* If you look at the clear cellophane package (similar to the ones used in vending machines for snack-sized portions of potato chips, pretzels, and such), all you see are a few lonely-looking chips lying forlornly at the bottom of the bag. The rest is just vacuum-sealed air.

Yes, I'm familiar with all the standard disclaimers—"Contents may have settled during shipping," "This package is sold by weight, not by volume." But trust me, the contents of this bag were settled to start with. And as for weight versus volume, the net weight of the SlimChips bag is quite revealing—the package tips the scales at a skimpy three-quarters of an ounce, well below the 1- to 1.25-ounce industry standard. The true extent of this silliness can be found on the back of the bag, where the nutritional information lists the product's basic serving size as one ounce. In other

NATURAL
CHOICES,
INC.

words, this bag they're selling you *isn't even a full serving.* Granted, a diet of SlimChips will probably have you slimming down in no time, but there has to be an easier way to lose weight than by rewarding this blatant flimflammery.

POCARI SWEAT REFRESHMENT WATER, 74-GRAM PACKET

O ne of the more amusing Japanese products is Pocari Sweat, a powdered beverage that serves as a Far East version of Gatorade. The product name is a little gross, but it's also refreshingly direct. After all, if you've been sweating all those salts and electrolytes out of your body, what better way to replenish them than with a product that explicitly identifies itself as sweat?

As interesting as the Pocari Sweat name may be, I'm more interested in a particular aspect of the package design. The 4.5-by-5.5-inch foil packet is adorned with a sweeping white wave clearly derived from the familiar Coca-Cola wave, one of the most institutionalized corporate graphics in the world. I believe the Coke wave is trademarked, so I can only assume the Coke folks don't yet know that their icon has been appropriated by a company marketing sweat. And I'm not going to tell them.

Pocari Sweat was sent to me by my friend Jodi, who used to down the stuff when she rowed for her college crew team. Her cover letter to me said, "In case you can't read Japanese, the instructions basically say that this packet should be mixed with one liter of water. Try it if you dare." I was game for this challenge until I noticed, to my amazement, a *freshness date* stamped onto the package—a date that had passed several months earlier. Sorry, but that's where I draw the line. It's one thing to drink sweat; it's another to drink *expired* sweat.

OTSUKA PHARMACEUTICALS

ANGOSTURA AROMATIC BITTERS, 4-OUNCE BOTTLE

E very bartender in the world has a cure for hiccups, and no two recipes are the same. But they have one thing in common: they all include bitters. A spoonful of bitters chased with a cup of water, bitters mixed with sugar, bitters drizzled over a lemon wedge, whatever. Why? Because a good hiccup cure generally involves a short, sharp shock to the system, and a small dose of bitters, as anyone who's ever consumed one can attest, is enough to send your system reeling clear across the room.

Bitters, an inconspicuous product even in its heyday, has become even more so in recent years. The cocktails that call for a dash or two of the stuff, like a Rob Roy or an Old-Fashioned, have fallen out of favor, leaving every bar in town with a dusty old bottle of bitters sitting on the back shelf, waiting for the next hiccup victim to emerge.

ANGOSTURA INTERNATIONAL

Just what's in bitters, anyway? Well, for starters, plenty of alcohol, at least according to the package label on Angostura bitters, the industry leader. Forty-five percent alcohol by volume, in fact, making bitters one of the most booze-intensive products you can buy at the supermarket. For a more specific breakdown, let's check out the ingredients listing: "Water, alcohol, gentian and harmless vegetable flavoring extracts and vegetable coloring matter."

You know you're in trouble when they have to put the word *harmless* in there to reassure you. Unfettered bitters, as you may have had the bad fortune to discover, is nasty with a capital N. Predictably, however, the Angostura label, which is packed with fine-print detail, would have us believe otherwise. Here we learn that aside from the obligatory drink recipes, this product has a bevy of uses, most of them inexplicably centering on food: "It has long been recognized as a pleasant and dependable stomachic. As a stimulant for the appetite, one to four teaspoonfuls before meals is suggested. . . . Because of its delightful flavour and aroma . . ."—are we talking about the same product here?—". . . it imparts an exquisite flavour to soups, salads, vegetables, sauces, fish, grapefruit, jellies, sherberts, ice cream, puddings, mince pies, and apple sauce." Damn, I *knew* there was something missing from the dessert bar at that restaurant last night.

Incredibly, the whole hiccup-cure angle is completely absent; perhaps the Angostura folks feel such a utilitarian task is beneath them. On one front, however, they cannot be faulted: here is a product that truly lives up to its name.

HYDROX COOKIES, 16-OUNCE PACK

There are really only two kinds of people in this world. The problem is coming up with the definitive way of sorting them out: Republicans vs.

Democrats? Beatles fans vs. Stones fans? Lefties vs. right-ies? Innies vs. outies? Bowlers vs. golfers?

These are all good litmus tests, but they tend to leave certain crucial variables unaccounted for. For my money, if you're looking for a quick, shallow way to oversimplify and neatly categorize someone's identity, only one standard will do: *Oreo people vs. Hydrox people.*

SUNSHINE
BISCUITS, INC.

Personally, I think Hydrox just taste better than Oreos—they're less cloyingly sweet, their flavor less synthetic. Moreover, Oreos have a sort of semigloss finish that bugs me—it seems so obviously artificial—while Hydrox have a simple matte surface. Then there's the issue of structural integrity: I've found Oreos to be more brittle, more likely to break apart when I'm separating the sandwich sections to get at the interior filling.

Such distinctions may be self-evident to me, but you'd be surprised (okay, no you wouldn't) to learn how few people have devoted serious thought to the Oreo/Hydrox dichotomy. The two cookies are very similar visually (for the record, Oreos are a sixteenth of an inch wider in diameter), and most folks tend to think of them as the same animal. This perception clearly favors Oreos, since they now control 87 percent of the chocolate sandwich cookie market. And with the Nabisco monolith behind them, Oreos are pretty well guaranteed to maintain a higher public profile, too. All of which must be rather frustrating if you're in the marketing department at Hydrox's parent company, Sunshine Biscuits. How do you successfully market a product that's perceived to be more or less equivalent to another, better-known product?

"The challenge is monumental to say the least," said Sunshine Marketing Vice President Gerry Jantzi, who was nice enough to discuss Hydrox with me for the better part of an hour. Faced with an uphill battle, Jantzi said Sunshine tries a mixture of in-store couponing, competitive pricing by market, point-of-sale signage, and back-to-school promotions targeted at the crucial youth market. In other words, all the usual nickel-and-dime tricks of the trade, none of which is likely to trigger a significant shift in the hyper-competitive cookie marketplace.

Jantzi's pitch is almost exclusively pro-Hydrox, with barely a hint of anti-Oreo sentiment (when asked how he'd convince a cookie-ignorant space alien that Hydrox are the superior brand, he replied, "I'd just have him taste the product"). Personally, I think he should consider a more aggressive approach — negative campaigning may not be pretty, but it works in politics, right? For example, based on what Jantzi told me, Hydrox have a significant advantage in terms of creme filling (so spelled, per industry standard, because there's no actual cream in it): the filling accounts for 34 percent of a Hydrox cookie's weight, compared with only 27 percent for an Oreo. Why not trumpet this fact a bit more loudly? No wonder Nabisco had to develop and market their filling-enhanced DoubleStuf Oreos in 1975 — they were barely offering any filling to begin with.

Maybe the problem is in the name. Let's face it, there isn't much you can do with a product name like Hydrox (although Sunshine tried a decade or so ago with that embarrassing "Hi, Drox!" ad campaign). The Hydrox name was born in 1908, when Sunshine founders Joseph Loose and John Wiles, having already developed the concept for America's first creme-filled sandwich cookie, were trying to come up with a product moniker that would complement the Sunshine name. The conversation apparently went something like this:

Loose: "Well, John, what goes with sunshine?"

Wiles: "Let's see, Joe. Hey, I know — water! *Water* goes with sunshine! You know—they're both elements of nature and all that."

Loose: "Dang, you're right, John. Now, uh, let's think for a minute here. Well, water is wet, it's a liquid, it's made of hydrogen and oxygen . . ."

Wiles: "That's it, Joe! Don't you see? *Hyдr*ogen and *oxy*gen— *Hyдrox*!"

While this may seem like a better way to name a cleaning fluid than a cookie (my friend Jim eschews Hydrox for precisely this reason), it nonetheless came to pass that Wiles and Loose used the periodic table of elements as the basis for their product's name. This may have made their high school chemistry teachers proud, but it wasn't enough to corner the market. The copycats at National Biscuit introduced the Oreo in 1912, flexed their superior promotional muscle, and that was the way the cookie crumbled.

Not that Sunshine has thrown in the towel, mind you. Jantzi said the company, whose ovens pump out 5.1 million Hydrox each day and 13.5 million pounds of Hydrox per year, is pursuing a number of strategies to make the Hydrox name more visible, including a licensing deal for a Hydrox Cookies 'n' Cream ice cream bar. Still, even this development underscores some of the problems Hydrox are up against. When I asked Jantzi if any ice cream brands— Breyers or Sealtest, say—currently use Hydrox in their basic cookies 'n' cream flavors, he said yes, but the companies in question have asked not to be named. Apparently they're afraid of being publicly associated with the less popular, lower-profile Hydrox name, preferring to let the consumer mistakenly assume they're using Oreos. And as long as this sort of spineless "support" remains the norm, Hydrox's relative outsider status will remain a self-fulfilling prophecy. As Jantzi put it, frustration evident in his voice, "It's a David and Goliath scenario."

I t's amusing to see how General Mills is working both sides of the consumer street with its Cheerios product line. Original Cheerios, which date back to 1941 (when they were known as Cheeri-Oats), are now promoted as one of the more harmless mass-market cereals — simple, basic, only one gram of sugar per serving, rarely any free toy inside the box, no cartoon animal mascot, plenty of oat bran, no extraneous bells or whistles. It's worth remembering, however, that when we were all growing up, before the whole health-consciousness thing kicked in, Cheerios weren't admirable or respectable or back-to-basics — they were just boring.

But by playing up the low-sugar angle and then reaping an unexpected windfall when the oat bran craze fell into their laps, the General Mills folks have been able to reinvent Cheerios as a cereal parents across America can serve to their kids without too much residual guilt.

General Mills made a token attempt to reposition Cheerios among the larger community of junk-food cereals in 1979, when they launched Honey Nut Cheerios (sugar up the wazoo, plus an animated bee mascot). Paradoxically, however, it was the "sugar bad, oat bran good" mania of the 1980s that truly paved the way for Cheerios' move toward the sweetened holy land. With the oat bran fad providing a wholesome cachet to the Cheerios name, General Mills was free to expand the brand's parameters, especially in terms of the sucrose factor. This marketing pitch became apparent with the 1988 debut of Apple Cinnamon Cheerios (current print ads for which depict a big jar of brown sugar) and continued with the 1991 appearance of Multi-Grain Cheerios (which, in spite of their healthful-sounding name, have six times the sugar of regular Cheerios). By trading on the consumer goodwill generated by traditional Cheerios, General Mills was able to create a product line that could be virtually all things to all cereal eaters.

GENERAL MILLS, INC.

The latest and presumably final step in this sequence is Frosted Cheerios, which arrived on supermarket shelves late in 1995. I'm sure this product was in development for years, so it's surprising to see the package look like such a rush job. The graphics on the front and back panels are remarkably lackluster, with the super-enlarged images of the frosted *o*s themselves looking more like decaying industrial ruins than a breakfast cereal. Even worse, the General Mills copywriting staff appears to have been on vacation—one bit of failed hype claims that Frosted Cheerios offers "one great taste after another, and another, and another . . ." while a blurb on the side panel says they're "crunchy, sweet, and so good, so good, so good." Welcome to the scratched-record school of marketing.

As for the taste, my friend Tom put it best: "They taste just like Alpha-Bits—only every letter is an *o*."

GRENADE THERMOGENIC ENERGY DRINK, 22-OUNCE BOTTLE

T he cold war may be over, but paramilitary aesthetics never go completely out of fashion. The latest evidence of this is Grenade, an energy drink designed to provide peak performance to gym rats during workouts. The beverage, which was launched in early 1995 by Nature's Best, is packaged in an olive-drab container shaped like a shell casing. An army-style stencil typeface adds to the effect, and the cap, which features a grenade-esque pull strip, provides just the right touch of interactivity.

And then, of course, there's the name. According to Nature's Best president Hal Katz, the company and its ad agency, Waring & LaRosa, went through quite an assortment of potential product names before settling on Grenade. "We were trying to play around with some sort of energy word," he explained, "so we tried a lot of 'turbo' words, a lot of 'nitro' words." When "Grenade" presented itself, said Katz, it seemed like the ideal solution, since it provided the desired energy motif and could also be broken down into a beverage-associated "-ade" word, like "lemonade."

Waring & LaRosa's print ad for the drink, however, dispenses with the beverage angle and brings the product's munitions-based subtext to the fore. It shows an actual hand grenade side by side with a 22-ounce bottle of Grenade. The weapon is captioned, "Warning: Contains an enormous amount of explosive energy"; the drink, "Ditto." In the unlikely event that anyone's missing the point, the body copy concludes with, "Hey, if you want to battle the competition, bring out the heavy artillery."

Katz seemed genuinely surprised when asked if he thought some consumers might object to the product's armament-oriented pitch. "A lot of people at gyms are ex-military people," he said. "Anyway, it's all taken in fun. It's more of a beverage-type name than a grenade-type name." Just in case you missed that little sleight

Nature's Best

of hand, let's try it again: Grenade is *not* a grenade-type name. Get it?

Katz, while pointing out that response to Grenade at military bases has been "spectacular," said Nature's Best has no plans to pursue any sort of cross-promotional deals with military manufacturers. And he specifically ruled out any tie-ins with G.I. Joe — seemingly a natural vehicle to reach potential Grenade consumers at a very early age — because Grenade "is not suitable for youngsters."

The reason for that, of course, is that Grenade is loaded with sugar and caffeine (as well as a variety of extracts and bodybuilding ingredients like Citrimax and white willow bark), which means it would reduce the average kid to little more than a blur. It apparently packs a sizable wallop for adults as well — Katz strongly advised against downing Grenade just before bedtime, but suggested that the drink could be used instead of coffee as a morning pick-me-up. Just picture it: " 'Morning, honey. Gimme a Grenade, will ya?"

SATHERS STUDENT FOOD, 2.5-OUNCE PACK

Back in the mid-1970s, the folks at Purina ran a commercial full of barnyard animals in an attempt to demonstrate that they weren't just a dog-and-cat company. The commercial showed, say, a goat, and then explained that Purina made Goat Chow. By the end of the spot, we'd learned that Purina also made Rabbit Chow, Pig Chow, Horse Chow, Donkey Chow, and just about every other sort of chow you could imagine. With Purina's wide-ranging zoological acumen thus affirmed, you were supposed to feel all the more confident when buying their Cat Chow for your tabby.

I don't know if Purina is still feeding every animal in the menagerie, but it doesn't much matter now that I've discovered Sathers Inc., a Minnesota outfit that takes chow to levels Purina never even thought of. I only have one Sathers product in my possession, but it's almost a product line unto itself: a snack-sized packet of trail mix—complete with raisins, peanuts, sunflower seeds, you know the deal—that's officially designated as *Student Food*. Hey, when you consider some of the ridiculous trendy pets that have been embraced at one time or another in this country (potbellied pigs, Akitas, rocks), students sound like the next logical step. And now, thanks to Sathers, we have the proper food to feed them. I bet they'll even eat out of your hand.

Of course, it's one thing to say students make fashionable pets, but the larger question is whether they make *good* pets. As someone who works for a living, I must admit I like the idea of taking an undergraduate out on a leash or directing a doctoral candidate to the litter box; I also like the image of a bowl of water and a bowl of Sathers Student Food sitting side by side in the corner of the kitchen. But I think it ultimately comes down to how well the little beasts can be domesticated: if you can teach your pet student to wash the dishes, clean the bathroom, take out the garbage, turn out the light when leaving a room, or at least gather up all the empty beer cans, then you might be in for some decent companionship. But be warned —I hear they're *real* hard to train.

SATHERS, INC.

COORS ARTIC ICE BEER, 12-OUNCE BOTTLE

hose who bemoan the dumbing down of America will no doubt find their worst fears confirmed by Coors Artic Ice, a recent entry in the ice-beer sweepstakes. Take a close look at that product name — it's *Artic*, not *Arctic*. If you didn't notice the difference right away, well, don't worry — neither did about 20 people at a party where I was running around with a bottle of Artic Ice, yelling, "Look, look at this nonsense, look at what they're doing here!"

Eager to hear Coors's side of the story, I called the 800 number listed on the bottle and went over the ABC's of Artic Ice with a Coors consumer rep, who said the company has been flooded with calls on this issue. She explained that Artic Ice's spelling came about when the Coors crew discovered they couldn't trademark the name "Arctic Ice," so they settled for what they figured was the next best thing.

Interestingly, the form letter the rep mailed me a few days later makes no mention of the trademark issue. It does say, however, that Coors's marketing team "was looking for a name that would convey the qualities of the product: exceptionally full-bodied, smooth, bold and cold. The unique spelling is easily noticed, easily pronounced, and memorable." And in a press release included with the form letter, Coors brand director Jon Runge points out that "many familiar trademarks are creatively named, such as Absolut vodka, Cheez Whiz, Nestlé Quik, Kix cereal, etc."

Nice try. With the exception of Absolut, all of those products feature what I like to call "gadget names": their misspellings take playful, obvious liberties and make use of screwball letters like *q*, *x*, and *z* (which are also the three highest-valued letters in Scrabble, confirming their gadget value). The misspelling in Artic Ice, meanwhile, is neither playful nor obvious, and has absolutely zero gadget quotient. It's so subtle it seems like a mistake, which is why this is a failed product name, no matter what spin Coors tries to put on it.

There's one other noteworthy aspect of the Artic Ice package. The label on the bottle features an interesting holographic effect, presumably meant to simulate an ice cube's refractive properties. This feature, which I've never seen before on a beverage package, must cost a bundle at the manufacturing stage—imagine how Adolph Coors must squirm every time an Artic Ice drinker absentmindedly peels the painstakingly designed label off of the bottle, as so many of us do while drinking a beer. And herein may lie the real reason for the spelling imbroglio—after they shelled out for the snazzy holographic gimmickry, maybe they just couldn't afford the *c*.

SQUEEZE CONE VANILLA CANDY, 4-OUNCE TUBE

R emember a few years back when there was all that fuss about serial killer trading cards? Believe me, there are far more insidious products lurking about in our nation's candy stores. If the family-values brigade is really worried about the plummeting morals of America's youth, they ought to take a long, hard look at Squeeze Cone, a vanilla-flavored candy that makes the serial killer cards look wholesome by comparison. You've heard of candy corn? Well, this is candy *porn*.

Squeeze Cone, as its name implies, is squeezable, so it comes in a plastic tube. The tube itself, which is about five inches long, features an assortment of playful graphics but is otherwise no different from the standard tube used for, say, a medium-sized toothpaste package. Squeeze Cone's prurient appeal begins to manifest itself, however, in the tube's two-inch-long cap, a tapered, prow-like affair that lends an unmistakably phallic dimension to the overall package design. Or, in the words of almost everyone to whom I've shown this product, "Man, is that a sex toy or what?"

It gets better. When you remove the cap and squeeze, Squeeze Cone turns out to be a semiclear, viscous liquid that spurts out of the tube and bears a striking resemblance to—well, use your imagination. And as my friend Gerard remarked when I gave him a taste, "Hey, this is better than the real thing."

AMURAL
CONFECTIONS

If you can get past the libidinous subtext, the obvious way to eat Squeeze Cone, it seems to me, is to squeeze a bit onto your fingertip and then lick it off. The stuff is sort of sickly sweet, and I find it hard to imagine even the most sugar-obsessed kid downing it in large doses. According to the nutritional information on the package, however, the entire tube contains only three servings, which presents the extremely off-putting prospect of consuming *a third of a tube* of Squeeze Cone in one sitting. The very thought of this is much more offensive than any of the product's sexual overtones. As Potter Stewart once remarked, I may not be able to define obscenity, but I know it when I see it, and this is it.

ARTIFACTS

FIVE

I generally prefer to examine products that are still in production and available — antiques are interesting, but as a rule they fall outside my concept of consumerism. Occasionally, however, I encounter a discarded object that teaches me some sort of inconspicuously consumptive lesson, and it is to these items that the following section is devoted.

LOW-WATTAGE LIGHTBULB

I n the summer of 1988 I went to visit my friend Sam in Youngstown, Ohio, the prototypical dying steel town near the Pennsylvania border. He'd promised to bring me to one of Youngstown's abandoned steel mills, which seemed like a cool way to spend a day. As we arrived at the Youngstown Sheet & Tube Co.'s Brier Hill Works blast-furnace site, which had been shut down since 1977, the first surprise was how easy it was to just waltz on in. No fence, no gate, no guard dogs, just a rusty No Trespassing sign barely visible behind some bushes. The bigger surprise, especially in light of this easy access, was that the whole place seemed untouched — no graffiti, no remnants of parties by burnout high school kids. In New York, it's hard to imagine a large structure being abandoned for more than a day or two before being snapped up by squatters or turned into a crack house, but as Sam explained to me, "The mills are these gigantic symbols of why everyone's out of work. We'd rather just ignore 'em."

The place was a total Twilight Zone — 20 acres filled with huge, monolithic beasts of machinery, elaborate catwalks and ramps all over the place, the millstream still running through the facility, the whole site all rusty and falling apart. Sam explained that because there had been no such thing as 60-day notification for plant closings in 1977, the company basically broke the bad news to everyone by saying, "Uh, don't bother to

MANUFACTURER
UNLISTED

come to work tomorrow." As a result, *everything* was still intact 11 years later: clothes in the lockers, time cards in the time clocks, office supplies in the foreman's desk drawers — it gave new meaning to "the day the earth stood still."

Climbing around from turbo-blower to rail yard to water-tube boiler to hot-blast stove, I couldn't stop thinking about all the men it had taken just to build the place, to say nothing of all the men who'd worked there. All that labor, all that energy, all the lives and families built around this site — for what? Despite such lofty ruminations, I couldn't resist the urge to purloin a few objects — a metal sign, a clipboard full of papers, that sort of thing. But something felt incomplete. Looking overhead at a series of hallway lightbulbs, I started unscrewing and then shaking them until I found one that sounded like its filament was still intact. I got it home and sure enough, it worked. Nearly a decade of very selective use later, it still does. Not just an artifact, mind you, but a *functional* artifact — a small tribute to a place whose memory has tremendous impact on me, a small living piece of a mammoth industrial corpse.

PETROMETER "TYPE H" FUEL TANK GAUGE

A few years after visiting the Youngstown steel mill (see above), I found myself exploring another abandoned industrial site, this time the defunct Falstaff Brewery, which straddles the northernmost tip of the Illinois-Indiana border. As is so often the case with expeditions like this one, the operation proceeded with a military-like precision. Accompanied by a half dozen or so Chicago-based friends, armed with the requisite screwdrivers, wrenches, hacksaws, and cooler full of beer, I led a strike-force mission that breached the facility's walls. I outlined the strategy that resulted in our successful infiltration and ultimate occupation of the grounds. I forged my colleagues and myself into an elite unit that couldn't be stopped, even by the brewery's formidable defenses.

Okay, okay. I trespassed; I broke and entered.

Breaking and entering is the only way to accomplish anything when engaged in this type of endeavor. And really, it's not even very difficult. With a plant that's been shut down as long as this one (about 15 years), exterior barriers like fences and locks tend to be so rusted and poorly maintained that they barely put up a fight. The owner of the site is invariably either an absentee realtor, a bankruptcy court, or some fat cat getting tan in Florida, so you don't have to worry about contending with any hands-on security measures like guards or dogs. And it's a sure bet that the cops are too busy counting their bribe money and shaking down the local prostitutes for blow jobs to worry about who's messing around in the old factory. Even if the police are tipped off to your presence, they'll probably assume that the only people who'd be sneaking around in such a place are either high school kids getting high or some homeless indigents. Either way, their reaction is bound to be, "Goddamn morons—hope they get themselves killed in there. Serve 'em right."

While the more skittish among you might be worried about precisely this eventuality, the fact of the matter is that industrial ruins tend to be fairly safe. Obviously, you have to steer clear of badly rotted floorboards and resist the urge to stick your toe in that bucket of mystery goo, but at the same time remember that every staircase, rampway, and overpass in the joint was designed to support dozens of men at a time, not to mention lots of heavy equipment, which means you and a few associates can safely navigate even the most rust-encrusted route with little concern. The Falstaff

PETROMETER CORP.

place, as it turned out, threw very few hazards in our path, and after hopping a barbed-wire fence, scaling a small shed, and removing some brackets from the door to the main production building, we were in.

As we began making our way through six or seven stories of utter decay, I started to experience the familiar rush of industrial exploration. Here we were, walking where nobody had walked in well over a decade. The gigantic machines that served as the facility's infrastructure offered mute testimony to sagging profits, market consolidation, and, no doubt, labor strife. Soon I found myself characteristically obsessed with the ghosts of the countless construction teams, shift workers, and beer drinkers whose lives had been affected by what we saw before us.

Matters reached a peak on the fourth floor, where we found a shower room. Off in the corner was a small, battered toilet. Its isolation struck me as almost poignant, and I suddenly sensed the immense loneliness of the whole place embodied in this nondescript fixture. I'd been aimlessly throwing switches and pushing buttons the whole way — none had worked, of course — but here was an opportunity to let part of the brewery fulfill its intended function once again. Pleased with the notion of bringing at least one small piece of the facility back to life, if only for a few seconds, I approached the dilapidated porcelain throne, unzipped my fly, and took the most conceptually satisfying leak of my life.

Naturally, we pillaged. A sign here, a sprocket there, a few meter gauges — just enough things to remember the place by. Which leads me to the Petrometer, a narrow, yard-long gadget that I liberated from a wall on the first floor. Designed to measure the capacity in a fuel tank, the Petrometer features a series of stamped-metal calibration markings that are used to read the fluid level in a lengthy glass tube. Visually, it resembles a jumbo, heavy-duty thermometer. The metal casing that houses the whole assemblage is fire-engine red, a color made all the more appropriate by the installation date noted on the back of the product: February 14, 1939.

It seems fitting that this most romantic date will be forever linked in my mind to this most romantic industrial encounter. And with the Petrometer now mounted on my kitchen wall, I'm reminded every day that the installation date serves as a grounding point, as a way to make some of the brewery's ghosts become human. What did the men who installed the Petrometer do with their wives and girlfriends after work that evening? Who among them came home with flowers *and* chocolates for their sweeties? Did they first wash off the dirt from a hard day's toil in the very shower room we had visited? And how many of them, even after scrubbing away under the hot water, couldn't quite remove all of the grime from beneath their fingernails before holding their loved ones close on Valentine's Day?

THE BEST OF THE LOVIN' SPOONFUL LP

Some used records are worth buying on manufacturing values alone, and this one surely fits the bill. Back when this record was manufactured, in 1967, they really knew how to make records: *HEAVY.* The thick vinyl disc alone weighs more than a contemporary LP and jacket combined, and doubles as a bulletproof vest for when I'm walking through unsavory neighborhoods. Then there's the excellent gatefold jacket, which goes beyond the limits of simple card stock, forging into the realm of pasteboard; it swings open and closed with the force of a titanium steel door, and the mighty spine (with band and album

KAMA
SUTRA/MGM
RECORDS

names nicely centered, natch) is, like, three-eighths of an inch thick! Built to last, still looks like new, all in all a magnificently permanent symbol of material satisfaction. Slide this baby onto the shelf and all the other records have to *move over!* It hits the back wall with a reassuring "thud," and then you can happily go to sleep, secure in the knowledge that if your apartment burns down during the night, at least one of your possessions is certain to survive the inferno.

SAFE-DEPOSIT BOX

W hen I was a kid my father would periodically amuse me by bringing out some of his more valuable possessions. It might be some Indian-head pennies, an ancestor's jewelry, a stock certificate—whatever. After letting me fondle these treasures for an evening or two, he'd whisk them away again, explaining that they had to go back to some mysterious place called a "safe-deposit box."

A few decades later, in a world where most of what we own has been reduced to electronic data and our most valued material possessions are likely to be kept in boring self-service mini-storage sites, safe-deposit boxes remain totally cool.

Entire movie plots have been built around them; that will with the inheritance you're counting on is in one them; Laura Palmer on *Twin Peaks* kept her naughty erotic secrets in one of them.

In every bank, the routine is the same: it takes two keys to gain access to the box—one key held by the person renting the box, the other by the bank. Throughout the years, this ritual symbiosis has resulted in some unlikely relationships between members of the public at large and the more straight-and-narrow ranks of bank staffers. On one side you've got the general public, including adulterous housewives, debt-ridden gamblers, unscrupulous drug dealers, obscure small business owners cheating on their taxes, and petty thieves, any of whom might have good reason to rent a safe-deposit box; on the other, an army of pinstripe-suited number-crunchers. All brought together by these magical boxes.

This particular box, which I picked up at a local junk outlet, is a little rough around the edges but still a nice example of the form. The exterior is an autumnal maroon, with a crisp ecru stripe running around the perimeter of the top side and nice brass corner brackets holding the whole thing together. Long and flat, it measures 5 inches wide by 22 inches long by only 2 inches high—not unlike a jumbo carton of Marlboros. And when it came to protection of valuables, this battered old specimen clearly gave its all. As is always the case with such boxes, it must have been manufactured to be fireproof (in case the bank burned down or the Ruskies dropped the big one), but its makers neglected to make it *rust*proof, leaving the poor vessel vulnerable to the curse of oxidation, a fate to which it long since succumbed.

MANUFACTURER UNLISTED

The keys are gone, the lock no longer functional, but the door, which is hinged along the top side, swings open rather grudgingly, as if the box is still trying to be faithful to its twin missions of privacy and secrecy, as if it *knows* I'm not its rightful owner. Inside, two objects: a rubber band and a scrap of paper, the latter adorned with a series of numerical scribblings—"7^{00}," "5^{00}," "12^{00}." Small monetary values? Times of day? Who wrote these notations, and why? This small glimpse into the box's former life is enough to send my mind racing. The box is now alive, filled with stories of a family's history, of a bank patron's triumphs and failures. Sitting in my living room, this box no longer tries to guard its secrets. It wants to share them with me, to scream them out—but it can't find the words.

JELENKO JEWELRY KILN
DIXON ETCHING BURRS
HEART-SHAPED INSIDE FLAT BEZEL PLATES

This review is devoted to Phil Bayer, a retired machinist whom I first encountered when our block association organized a series of stoop sales one summer. Everyone else brought out the typical assortment of used books and old clothing, but Phil's stoop featured an unusual industrial thingie that caught my attention. Austere, black, quite heavy for its 5-by-7-by-10-inch dimensions, and featuring an interesting cantilevered door that opened to reveal a small compartment, it resembled a miniature safe, except that it also had a cute little gauge (to measure temperature? pressure?) up on top, and a cloth cord leading to a plug.

When Phil noticed me inspecting his merchandise, he rushed over and said, "Know what that is? Don't know, do ya?" When I confessed that I didn't, he proudly announced,

"It's a kiln." A jewelry kiln, for firing small enamel jobs. It had belonged to one of Phil's relatives, who'd been in the trade.

I was already hooked, but Phil wasn't sure he wanted to reel me in. "You don't make jewelry, do you?" he asked. When I explained that I admired the kiln as an interesting object, he frowned, rubbed his chin, and began muttering, "As an object . . . an object . . ." It wasn't too hard to guess his misgivings—he wanted the kiln's new owner to utilize this specialized tool, not turn it into a museum piece. I couldn't honestly say that I planned to go into the jewelry business, but after a bit of wrangling Phil grudgingly decided that perhaps I was worthy of the kiln after all. Twenty bucks later, it was mine.

• • •

The kiln was too heavy to tote around to the remaining stoop sales, so I just lugged it straight home and picked up where I'd left off. As I passed Phil's stoop, however, I noticed that he'd brought out something new: a small, cylindrical wooden capsule, about three inches high and two inches wide, with a top cover piece that fit onto a lower base piece. Like the kiln, it appeared to be at least 50 years old.

THE
JELRUS CO.,
INC.

I removed the cover from the base and was rewarded with the pleasing sight of 27 thin metal rods, each with a distinct nub at the top end, sticking up

out of the lower piece. Each rod was about an inch and a half long and sat in its own little hole that had been drilled into the base. The overall effect was of an industrial pincushion. Once again, I was thoroughly confused and thoroughly entranced.

"They're etching burrs," said Phil, who'd noted my return with a raised eyebrow. "They're like drill bits, for a special jewelry-finishing tool." The tool itself, which, again, had been used by Phil's jeweler relation, was gone, but I didn't much care—the burrs themselves, sitting in their nifty wooden canister, were about the coolest things I'd ever seen.

Phil didn't understand my enthusiasm. "You want these, too?" he asked. "What for?" He still didn't get it when I tried to explain, but this time he didn't resist. "Okay, go ahead—I didn't really think anyone would buy them." I raced home again, this time lighter by a ten-spot, and admired this prize of prizes.

MANUFACTURER ILLEGIBLE

•   •   •

When I returned to check out the rest of the stoop sales, Phil flagged me down. At this point I believe he'd identified me as "a live one."

"You know," he said, "I've got a basement full of stuff like this. Jeweler's tools, machinist's tools, all sorts of stuff. You wouldn't be interested in any of that, would you?" A big neon sign that said "Pay Dirt" clicked on in my brain.

I didn't have enough time that day to accept Phil's offer, but we traded phone numbers and agreed to talk again soon. Two weeks later, I found myself in his living room, his wife rolling her eyes as he regaled me with tales of his industrial career. After about half an hour of this, he finally led me to the basement, where it turned out that his oratory was just beginning. Phil had obviously been waiting a decade or three for someone to be interested in what he had to say, and now I was his captive audience. Surrounded by an impressive array of mechanical gadgetry, he barely knew where to start. For the next two hours he shared with me his considerable opinions about tungsten carbide drills, micrometers, the Precision Museum, oxyacetylene blowtorches, the Society for Industrial Archeology (see Chapter 6), the jeweler's lathe he hoped to sell for a few hundred bucks, the disappearance of trades and tradesmen, and other thoughts accumulated during a machinist's life.

I enjoyed listening to Phil, but I didn't want him to forget why I'd stopped by. When his batteries appeared to be running down, I reminded him that he'd promised to let me purchase some of his stash. And I knew just what I wanted, too. In the course of his monologues he'd shown me a bunch of small, thick, very industrial-looking metal plates, each one with a heart-shaped cutout in the center. These, Phil had explained, were stamping blanks for making heart-shaped lockets. Because lockets can come in many sizes, there were about a

dozen of the plates; better still, each one matched up with a corresponding heart-shaped stamping punch.

The contrast of the ubiquitous, Hallmark-esque heart against the plate's riveted, heavy-industrial face was irresistible. Phil didn't get it, but by now he'd learned to take my money without questioning my motives. After a bit of haggling, I handed Phil $75, shook his hand, and walked off with enough heart-shaped stuff to start my own Valentine's Day franchise.

Just as Phil never fully appreciated my affection for his objects, I think he might be disappointed by what I've done with them. They're displayed around my apartment, alongside all the other industrial totems that I like to use as home decor. And although I never tried to explain this to Phil, these items' appeal to me goes beyond the aesthetic — when I look at the kiln, for instance, I inevitably start to extrapolate, thinking of the plant that manufactured it, the now-defunct firm that peddled it, and all the people wearing jewelry that was fired in it. As satisfying as such ponderings may be, however, it seems a bit selfish to keep them to myself — other people should get a chance. All of which suggests that I'll be having one hell of a stoop sale myself some day.

SCORE-KING 50 CONTROLLED-WEIGHT BOWLING PIN

T his product, which I found in the trash outside a bowling facility, is a superior pin, far outdistancing the many others I own. To begin with, the finish on the plastic coating is superb: glossy, thick, clean, and with almost no fissures except where the pin itself has cracked. Perhaps more to the point, in the few spots where the finish *has* chipped off, it hasn't taken any of the underlying plastic or paint with it (a big problem on my cut-rate AMF Amflite pins). The Brunswick Mixer fares somewhat better in this regard, but it and the AMF model both have a pasty, almost sickly look and give a dull, one-color treatment to the American Bowling Congress crest, while the Score-King treats the hallowed logo to a splendid red-blue-black display. What's more, all AMF pins, as well as the cheaper Brunswicks, have those two red stripes ringed around the pin's neck, which is nice, but it's no contest when compared to the Score-King's far more attractive maroon crown wrapped around the same area of the pin. Finally, as befits such a top-shelf product, the Score-King is made of superior wood (maple, natch), far sturdier in the long run, and resulting in a much more satisfying, organic sound when inevitably knocked over by the cats.

BRUNSWICK BOWLING & BILLIARDS CORPORATION

TOAST-O-LATOR ELECTRIC TOASTER

When was it decided that two slices would constitute a proper, "normal" serving of toast? This question occurred to me recently after I saw an old one-slice toaster at a product design exhibit. The show's program notes repeatedly explained that most of the products on display were designed with planned obsolescence in mind, but the toaster made me wonder if another sort of consumer manipulation was at work. Did the eventual shift to two-slice toasters indicate that the appliance manufacturers had been in cahoots with the bakeries in an effort to increase bread sales?

If so, their scheming spelled a death sentence for the Toast-O-Lator, an amazing toaster that I picked up at a junk store. I've never seen anything else like it, and the reactions from my friends suggest that you probably haven't either. The Toast-O-Lator, originally marketed in the 1940s, doesn't exactly have a one-slice capacity — in fact, it theoretically has an *unlimited* capacity — but the logistics of its design definitely make it best suited to the one-slice toast consumer, which probably explains why it didn't survive in a two-slice market.

Here's the deal: The Toast-O-Lator, like so many midcentury toasters, features a chrome body atop a black Bakelite base, with all the classic teardrop-shaped curvatures and streamlined details that add up to a very attractive product. But it's the dimensions that are so unusual: 11 inches long by 10 inches high by only 3.5 inches wide. Stranger still, the Toast-O-Lator is not a top-loader. Instead, after flipping the power switch to "on," you put your slice of bread, positioned upright, into an opening at the left end of the appliance, where four rows of undulating teeth gently grab onto the bottom of the slice and take it on a slow "walk" through the Toast-O-Lator's body, which is wired with standard toasting filaments and coils. Think of it as a conveyor-belt ride through hell. The bread emerges as toast at the other end.

While this is tremendous fun—the bread looks like a giant inchworm as it moves along, and there's even a little portal located at mid-Toast-O-Lator, so that you can monitor your slice's progress as it moves by—it does become a rather high-maintenance proposition. If you leave the Toast-O-Lator unattended, your toast will fall out of the device when it completes its journey. If you have enough counter space, however, this problem can be surmounted by placing

your plate beneath the toast's egress point.

The multislice problem, unfortunately, is more troublesome. If you want more than once piece of toast, you have to put the first slice into the Toast-O-Lator and then wait for it to proceed nearly a slice-length's distance into the appliance before sending the second slice on its way, a wait that can last up to 30 very annoying seconds. I guess the nice thing, particularly if you're a toast glutton, is that you don't need to stop at two slices—you can repeat the routine ad infinitum, sending an endless flow of bread through the Toast-O-Lator to create the toast orgy of your dreams. The problem, of course, is that your dreams will be punctuated with 30-second delays.

TOAST-O-LATOR CO., INC.

As a devoted two-slice man myself, I find that the Toast-O-Lator's considerable charm evaporates in the face of this practical limitation. The American toast market apparently agreed, because the Toast-O-Lator Co., Inc., whose name leads one to believe it wasn't the most diversified of enterprises, is no longer in business. So there my Toast-O-Lator sits, on display in a corner of my kitchen, a victim of our culture's arbitrary two-slice dictum, while my late grandmother's two-slice, top-loading Sunbeam does all the work each morning.

McGILL HIGH-SPEED CHANGER

T his very satisfying change-making gadget, invented in the 1930s, first came to my attention back in the summer of 1969, when I became obsessed with its presence on our local Good Humor man's belt. It seemed like a particularly nifty device, especially to a five-year-old with no concept of banks, checks, or even paper currency—the guy just pressed on the little levers and out came a seemingly inexhaustible supply of coins. I liked the light-industrial sound that accompanied this activity—*ka-chunk, ka-chunk*—even better than the coins themselves. Not knowing exactly what the thing was called, I simply dubbed

it a "ka-chunker," a term I still use today.

Meanwhile, I had questions, many questions: Were the coins actually *being created* inside the gadget? If not, how did they get inside the device? Would the changer work for anyone, or did the Good Humor man possess some special technical skill that enabled him alone to dispense the coins? Could this skill be acquired by other grown-ups, or only by Good Humor vendors? And why did this particular gizmo look so perfect against the background of a white, crisply starched Good Humor uniform?

Today I have my own ka-chunker. I could have just bought a new one—they're still in production—but I was more interested in finding one with a history of its own. I finally located one in a junk shop and now I'm pondering a new series of questions: How much money ka-chunked its way through this object? Was it ever used by a Good Humor man? When did the pennies rack fall into near-total disuse, as it surely must have once vended products came under the pricing tyranny of five-cent increments?

Sturdy, timeless, ingeniously designed, and still fully functional, my ka-chunker looks great on my bedroom display shelf and makes an unbeatable accessory for low-stakes poker games ("I'll see your fifty cents . . ." —*ka-chunk, ka-chunk* —". . . and raise you seventy-five more . . ." —*ka-chunk, ka-chunk, ka-chunk*). Every now and then I run some change through it, which gets me thinking about the everyday beauty of coins. In an economy increasingly ruled by electronic transfers of funds, direct deposits, and credit card transactions, the ka-chunker serves as a handy reminder that cash isn't just liquid, but also *solid*.

J. M.
GALEF CO.

S ervices have their place in consumerism's grand scheme, but they nonetheless come in at the bottom of my economic totem pole — even the finest service-related pleasures don't offer the same sort of consumer tingle as a well-conceived, well-executed product. I mean, I genuinely like my barber — he's a nice guy, he's cheap, he's fast, he makes decent conversation, and he knows when I walk in that I want short back and sides — but what I really enjoy about a haircut is the *barber chair.* That said, here are some services and groups that have managed to push my buttons in inconspicuously consumptive ways.

My experience with the steel mill (see Chapter 5) marked the beginning of what has become a complete fascination with industrial design and decay, and those of you who don't yawn at the whole notion of such matters may be surprised to learn there's an organization devoted to this very obsession: the Society for Industrial Archeology, which was first brought to my attention by Phil Bayer (see Chapter 5). The SIA, according to its own literature, "promotes the identification, interpretation, preservation, and re-use of historic industrial and engineering sites, structures, and equipment."

A $35 annual SIA membership gets you a subscription to the quarterly *SIA Newsletter*, where the feature stories run along the lines of "Rare Corps of Engineers Photographs Discovered" and "Big Chattanooga Truss Bridge Restored." You'll also get the latest issue of the Society's juried research journal, *IA*, recent editions of which include such treats as "19th-Century Charcoal Production in Vermont," "Small-Scale Brickmaking in New Hampshire," and "The Introduction of Cast and Wrought Iron in Bridge Building."

Once you sign up with the national SIA, you'll also be invited to spend an additional $5 to join one of the local SIA chapters, which typically organize field trips to historic industrial sites. I'm sure the SIA would frown upon my penchant for finding my own sites, sneaking into them, and making off with a few well-chosen totems, but fortunately I see nothing in the bylaws about membership revocation. Anyone with even the slightest interest in how industry has shaped and affected our lives, regardless of technical or engineering training (I've got none myself), will find the SIA worth their while. Plus you get to walk around saying,

"I'm an industrial archeologist," which works better than you'd think at parties.

GRAND CANYON NATIONAL PARK

I really can't get too excited about the Southwest aesthetic. The whole adobe-and-turquoise deal does absolutely nothing for me, all that Spanish-influenced stuff just isn't my bag, and I have an inherent distrust for places where palm trees and cacti outnumber dogwoods and maples. But when circumstance recently offered me the fairly spontaneous opportunity to accompany a friend to Phoenix and then to the Grand Canyon, I figured sure, why not?

I've always been a lazy researcher, and this definitely extends to my travel habits. Although I'd dutifully purchased a copy of *Fodor's Arizona* a week or so before leaving New York, I never did get around to opening it at any point prior to or during the trip. So as we drove a rental car from Phoenix to the Canyon, I tried to take mental inventory of everything I knew about this natural wonder we were about to encounter. Unfortunately, my GC memory banks seemed to be stocking nothing but a few random scenes from that particularly loathsome Canyon-oriented episode of *The Brady Bunch* (the image of Alice being stuck with the ornery mule remains absurdly clear). With this meager store of knowledge serving as a loose contextual framework, I figured I was as prepared as I'd ever be to come face to face with what Howard the Duck once referred to as "this hole."

NATIONAL PARK SERVICE

Howard may have been a tad cynical, but I must admit that the Canyon completely failed to overwhelm me.

143

Impressive? Sure. Beautiful? Obviously. But divinely revelatory? Well, no. I was a bit ashamed of this reaction, since you always hear that the GC is supposed to inspire all sorts of awestruck wonder, until I compared notes with my travel partner and discovered she was experiencing precisely the same mixed emotions.

This eased the tension considerably—happily declaring ourselves a pair of typically jaded New York smart-asses, we thoroughly enjoyed the rest of the day, most of which we spent sipping Budweisers while perched at various spots along the GC's East Rim. By the end of the afternoon, the ambivalence I'd felt earlier had vanished. The Canyon and I had come to terms with each other, establishing a casual rapport I can only describe as friendship.

Incidentally, the aforementioned Budweisers proved to be the most crucial accessories we brought along. Sure, binoculars are nice, and of course you'll bring your camera, but if you want a really hot tip for your GC expedition, invest in a small cooler and a six-pack. I'm happy to report that the Grand Canyon makes a spectacular backdrop for drinking, and while everyone else is obsessively fiddling with their zoom lenses, you can be raising a toast to Mama Nature. Plus, after a few Buds you'll be ready to engage, however discreetly, in one of the truly sublime pleasures the Canyon offers: pissing over the edge.

FERRELL REED COMPLIMENTARY BUTTON SERVICE

 o I'm out thrift-shopping one day when I come across this very handsome dress shirt bearing the Ferrell Reed label. Nice red-black-blue striping on an ecru ground, looks as good as new, and my size to boot.

So I get it home, take it out and admire it for a minute or two, and I notice the following notation on the care label: "CALL 800-421-6119 EXTRA BUTTONS."

Now, it so happened that I had no immediate need for extra buttons on this or any other shirt, but I'd never heard of a complimentary button service, so I was intrigued. I got on the phone, called the number, and had a very nice chat with the charming Diane Johnson at Ferrell Reed, who confirmed that the haberdasher's policy is to provide extra shirt buttons (and collar stays, for that matter) to any customer in need of them.

"Ferrell likes his customers to be as happy as they can be," she explained. I contemplated whether to tell Diane that Ferrell Reed had *already* made me very happy by designing a beautiful, expensive shirt that someone bought and then gave to Goodwill, where I found it for two bucks, but I figured this might not go over too well, so I decided to keep it to myself.

Diane promised to send me the company's full range of button offerings, and she was also kind enough to toss in some Ferrell Reed promotional literature. As a result, I now know that Mr. Reed collects classic cars, sits on the board of the National Neckwear Association, and got his big break when he landed a job selling menswear at "the finest store in Salt Lake City." In what I'm sure is an unbiased, objective assessment, he is described as a man who is "serious about work but always finds time to laugh and love life"; my own unbiased, objective assessment of his photograph in one of the promo brochures is that his big facial-hair influence was Leroy Neiman.

As for the buttons, well, they're your basic plastic shirt buttons, produced in a subtle variety of off-white shades. Nothing to get too excited about, but hey, they're free. And now that I've given you the toll-free phone number, you don't even have to own a Ferrell Reed shirt to get in on the deal.

COLD TRAIL MAIL CO.

You say you're hiding from creditors? Mobsters looking to fit you with a set of cement footwear? Uncle Sam all over your ass about those back taxes? Maybe you need a stealthy, untraceable way of mailing a letter bomb, a ransom note, or some crystal meth?

Any way you slice it, the Cold Trail Mail Co. has just what you need. If you want a phony address, they'll set one up for you; if you want your mail sent out with an evasive postmark so that it can't be traced back to you, they'll do that, too. And if you're thinking that this all sounds no different than what Mail Boxes Etc. offers, here's the kicker: Cold Trail is located in a town called Wasilla. That's in *Alaska,* kids.

As Cold Trail's brochure explains, "Alaska is remote in both distance and communications networks. . . . The majority of the state is accessible only by air or sea, and the climate is challenging. When you send or receive mail via Alaska, your correspondents will likely assume you are here. IF EVASION IS YOUR GOAL, ALASKA IS THE PERFECT DETERRENT!"

So what does this mean in practical terms for a postal customer who wants to be, shall we say, discreet? Well, for $15 a month, Cold Trail will provide you with an Alaskan P.O. box address. Everything you receive there will be forwarded to you at no additional charge. If you want to send out mail with an Alaskan postmark, Cold Trail will mail your presealed, prestamped letters for a dollar a pop, or a flat $5 charge for as many letters as you can fit into a manila envelope. They'll also mail your prewrapped, prestamped packages for $5 each.

Cold Trail was founded by Mary Place, who says she

imagines her typical customers to be "divorced people, people who maybe owe a lot of child support but want to write to their kids without being found." She stresses, however, that this is mere speculation on her part—she basically follows a "don't ask, don't tell" doctrine, and adds, "I don't imagine anyone would confide in me anyway." She's had only moderate response to the small classified ads she's run in *High Times, Soldier of Fortune,* and a variety of detective magazines (which is where I first encountered her), but hopes to branch out into international service by attracting an overseas partner. Essentially offering a big, friendly rock to hide under, Cold Trail Mail puts the "inconspicuous" in inconspicuous consumption.

INVENTION SUBMISSION CORPORATION

T hose of you with creative urges may be interested in the services offered by the Invention Submission Corporation, a Pittsburgh-based firm that acts as a broker between inventors and small companies looking to invest in tomorrow's craze today.

If you plan on engaging ISC's services, the first thing you may want to invent is a good counterfeiting machine—the company's efforts do not come on the cheap. For a cool $625, they'll create a "Basic Information Package"—essentially an attractively packaged résumé—for your invention. If you want them to shop your idea around at trade shows, in product registries, via press releases, in data banks, and so on, it'll run you another $700 to $7,000—fees of sufficient heft to make the casual inventor think twice about the whole thing.

The image of the inventor as a nerdy recluse who puts his

family through hell while creating an endless succession of defective kitchen appliances may be a stereotype, but most stereotypes have a basis in truth, and the people at ISC definitely know who their potential clients are. ISC's promotional brochure reads like a self-esteem primer for frustrated creative types, studded with encouraging little pick-me-ups like, "There are no restrictions on inventors. . . . They are wealthy and poor, educated and self-taught," and, "One little-known fact is that more individual inventors than corporations have been responsible for the major inventions of this century," and my favorite, "Your friends and relatives might not take your idea seriously; we will."

ISC took me so seriously, in fact, that all it took was one exploratory call to their offices to land me on their "active" list. For the most part their communiqués were just of the "We hope you received the information you requested" variety, but things got pushy when a fellow from the ISC offices phoned me at home as I ate my dinner one evening and, after exchanging a few pleasantries with me, started badgering me for details.

"What exactly *is* your invention?" he inquired. Not having one to discuss, I slipped into my notion of a paranoid-inventor persona: "Um, I'd really rather not describe it. I just don't think I'm ready to talk with you about it yet. Okay?"

Undaunted, he persisted. "Do you have a model?" he asked. "Have you gone so far as to prepare a prototype? We'd love to see it, you know."

"Look," I screamed into the receiver, *"I'd really rather not talk to you about it just yet! Okay?"* At this point, and only at this point, did my ISC contact agree that this was indeed okay. Ten days later, however, I received another mailing from ISC, asking if I'd received all the materials I'd requested and adding, "We tried to telephone you recently but failed to reach you." I think this was a typo — they must have meant that they'd failed to *breach* me.

THE AMERICAN WATCH CO.

I couldn't tell you which is cooler — my 1961 Nathan's Famous ashtray or my 1975 Hershey's with Almonds paperweight — but I do know why they're both so captivating: It's fun to see a familiar logo where we don't expect to see it, and as consumers we find it inviting to allow a merchandised logo to institutionalize a product's existence in our minds. And while Hershey's and Nathan's are still ongoing enterprises, it's worth noting that the same cannot be said of the firm behind my Red Star Soda bottle opener. And herein lies the true value of identity merchandising — long after your company has gone belly-up, it can live on, immortalized, in the form of merchandised spin-off products.

But why should big corporations get to have all the fun? Why not institutionalize — and thus immortalize — something nobody's ever heard of? My plan was to merchandise the logo for my fanzine, *Beer Frame: The Journal of Inconspicuous Consumption.* The possibilities seemed limitless: I would create *Beer Frame* T-shirts, *Beer Frame* bumper stickers, *Beer Frame* coffee mugs, *Beer Frame* baseball caps, *Beer Frame* refrigerator magnets, *Beer Frame* golf balls; I would merchandise the concept of inconspicuous consumption until it became too conspicuous to ignore.

Unfortunately, these dreams of world conquest were soon dashed upon the rocks of fiscal reality. As I quickly discovered in the pages of several merchandising catalogs, you can have your logo slapped onto just about anything, or even have it stamped into a chocolate bar, but the minimum order for each item tends to run in the $500 range — peanuts for a legit company running a promotion, but far beyond what I had in mind.

Soon thereafter, I found myself on an airplane, thumbing

through one of those in-flight magazines. To my surprise, there were ads from four different companies peddling customized wristwatches, each one offering to print anyone's logo onto a few sample watches for a low introductory price. If you liked the results, you could buy dozens more at a higher rate. Since I only wanted a few watches in the first place, this was exactly what I was looking for.

I chose the cheapest deal, which was proffered by the American Watch Co. They promised a 15-day turnaround on up to eight watches for $14 each, plus a $4 shipping fee. I made a stat of the *Beer Frame* logo, wrote a check, and prepared a suitably businesslike cover letter. Two weeks later I was the proud owner of eight water-resistant, quartz-movement *Beer Frame* watches. They keep perfect time, and the logo looks great. Best of all, every time I wear one of them I feel that tingle of institutionalized immortality, the magic of conferred legitimacy. Other people feel it, too—almost without exception, anyone who sees my *Beer Frame* watch says, "Hey, cool—where can I get one of those?"

By the way, if you're not into the notion of identity graphics but just think it would be cool to have a custom-made watch, these companies essentially offer you the chance to design your own timepiece. Choose or create a graphic element that you think would look nifty on a watch face—an abstract design, a clipping of your favorite cartoon character, a dupe of your tattoo, whatever—and just claim that it's your logo. Believe me, if the service I received is any indication, these companies are so desperate for business that they'll gladly slap *anything* on a watch without thinking twice.

Finally, while it's plenty of fun to merchandise something that almost nobody else knows about, like *Beer Frame*, I bet it's even more fun to merchandise something that's never even existed in the first place. Design your own logo for a fictitious product or service, flash the resultant watch to friends and colleagues, and before you know it you'll have created a demand for something with no supply.

FIREFOX ENTERPRISES

eed a 100-pound drum of magnesium? Maybe 40 gallons or so of HX-878 propellant bonding agent, direct from NASA's surplus stock? How about a few dozen plastic spherical shell casings? And have you checked your supply of isophorone diisocyanate curing agent lately?

Whatever your pyrotechnic needs, you'll probably find what you're looking for in the pages of the Firefox Enterprises catalog. Serving a market primarily composed of special-effects professionals, magicians, state and local police departments, rocketry clubs, and, one imagines, arsonists, Firefox has just about everything imaginable for any application that involves touching a match to a fuse, from custom-milled oxidizers and propellant resins to ignition materials and smoke mixtures.

None of which is to suggest that Firefox will just blithely sell you all the necessary ingredients for you to create your own private stock of M-80s. Unless you have a federal explosives permit, they won't ship you combinations of chemicals that are "obviously intended to be used for constructing flashpowder and/or exploding fireworks devices . . . and other illegal audible effects devices." They'll also keep tabs on your ordering history to see if you're trying to assemble a munitions depot on the installment plan. On the other hand, they tell you exactly how to apply for the necessary permit, and if you're approved, they'll happily "furnish chemicals and materials in any quantity or combination you may require." Bingo.

Firefox's appeal ranges far beyond the pyromaniacal. The company stocks a wide variety of model rocket and missile supplies, including motors, tubing, aerodynamic fins, and recovery parachutes. In addition, they carry assorted tools and supplies, laboratory equipment, and "exotic hardware," the latter of which is best exemplified by a pest-control grenade launcher. They also offer a literature section, featuring such titles as *Deluxe Bottle Rockets* and *Smoke Generation: Tactical/Survival/Civilian,* although it's hard to imagine any of this printed matter surpassing the fun of the catalog itself. Even if you're not equipped or inclined to use any of Firefox's wares, some of the descriptions alone are priceless. I'm sorely tempted, for example, to drop $33 on a 30-meter roll of Thermalite igniter cord, which is available in three different burn rates (16, 8, or 5 seconds per foot) and is described as being ideal for rocket motor ignition or "general-purpose use." Whatever that is.

Despite all the stern language in the catalog about the company's refusal to ship incendiary combinations of materials, at least one chemistry-minded Firefox customer, who happens to be an acquaintance of mine, has had little difficulty obtaining the proper components to make his own illegal firecrackers. Wanna get in on the fun? Don't wait until the Fourth of July—get Firefox's catalog and put their goods to the test.

THE ACCOMMODATION PROGRAM

T he Accommodation Program, one of the more amusing scams whipped up by the friendly propagandists at Philip Morris, shows just how far the tobacco lobby has fallen in this anti-smoking era. Essentially a desperate promotional gimmick to convince the hospitality industry to maintain fast-dwindling smoking sections in restaurants, hotels, arenas, malls, and airports, the Accommodation Program centers around a red and green glyph captioned with the message, "Nonsmokers and smokers welcome here." Of course, non-smokers are already welcome everywhere, so the whole point of the program is contextual, to give smoking some level of respectability by association.

PHILIP
MORRIS U.S.A.

The Accommodation symbol itself (which Philip Morris would not allow to be reproduced in this book) is a remarkable triumph of wishful thinking. Derived from the Chinese yin-yang design, it presents smoking and non-smoking — and hence smokers and non-smokers — as equal partners in a harmonious social balance. But according to the industry's own data, only 25 percent of adult Americans light up, which means the symbol's proportions are badly out of whack.

For those of you who enjoy interactive participation, however, the Accommodation Program actually allows you to play along. If you call Philip Morris and ask for info on the campaign, as I did, you'll receive a packet containing two sets of small stickers. The first, intended for use in establishments that permit smoking, includes a laudatory salutation and a promise of continued patronage ("Thank you for accommodating non-smokers and smokers. You can count on my business in the future"), while the second set, to be used in smoke-free businesses, turns the economic message into a threat ("I noticed you don't provide smoking accommodations. . . . If you'd like my business in the future, please accommodate smokers"). Philip Morris recommends that the stickers be placed on the receipt or guest check when you're paying the tab, but that doesn't sound like much fun. If you really want to spread the gospel of tubercular goodwill, I suggest putting the stickers on plates, silverware, your waiter's forehead, or any other spot that presents itself. After all, accommodation is as accommodation does.

VAN DYKE SUPPLY COMPANY

Face it, you need a new hobby. That stamp-collecting thing is getting a bit old, don't you think? And please, enough with the gardening, woodworking, painting, knitting, hiking, model making, boating, whittling, and photography—totally passé, each and every one of 'em. You need something new. You need something exciting. You need taxidermy.

Don't laugh. Skinning and mounting a dead animal might not sound like your idea of fun, but a good 75,000 or so professional and amateur American taxidermists would disagree with you, and the number is growing. That information comes from L. J. Van Dyke, and he ought to know—his mail-order operation has been servicing the trade for nearly half a century.

The Van Dyke's catalog, which runs nearly 300 pages, is practically an education in taxidermy. The company stocks all the necessary materials for you to create your own taxidermed menagerie. Step right up and name your animal—chances are Van Dyke's carries a sculpting form for it. In addition to the obvious deer and moose, they'll fix you up with everything you need to work on, say, a warthog, antelope, seal, wildebeest, raccoon, otter, porcupine, caribou, armadillo, lynx, beaver, wild hog, or kangaroo.

The most spectacular items in the catalog are the dozens of glass eyes, which are available for a multitude of mammals, birds, fish, reptiles, and amphibians. The most obvious comparison would be marbles, but these genuinely beautiful orbs, many of them sparkling and shimmering, are really more like jewelry. And at prices averaging only a few bucks per pair, you can buy a pile of them just to keep around the house.

Less beautiful than the eyes, but every bit as interesting, are the other assorted artificial body parts that Van Dyke's sells: noses, antlers, whiskers, claws, mouth/jaw assemblies ("Look at the throat muscles in these jaw sets!" says the catalog), ears, tails, and so on. The idea behind all this is apparently that you can never be sure just which part of your four-legged trophy will be destroyed or damaged by the buckshot and therefore have to be reconstituted, but I see other possibilities. With this much animal anatomy available, there's really very little need to go hunting—you can create your own beast from scratch.

In case you don't already have your own taxidermy equipment, Van Dyke's handles a wide variety of highly specialized tools of the trade. An electric gizmo called a "bird and small mammal degreaser and flesher" will run you $139.95, but the handheld ear opener ("Greatly improved!") is only $9.45.

Interestingly, Papa Van Dyke finds taxidermy uniquely suited to today's ecologically and environmentally sensitive times. "People are more conscious of wantin' to preserve things," he told me, with absolutely zero hint of irony. "Years ago they'd just eat the damn thing and forget about it." I considered suggesting that perhaps the best way to preserve a deer, bear, moose, or whatever would be to avoid shooting it in the first place, but something told me I wouldn't get the most appreciative response.

Okay, so let's say you like the sound of all this, but you have no taxidermy experience and don't know where to begin. No problem—Van Dyke's has the training materials to get you started, from instructional manuals (*Fish Mounting, Oily Skinned Varieties*, $9.95) to books (*Taxidermy Pricing Workbook*, $39.95) to videos (*Skinning and Prepping a Small Mammal for Mounting*, $24.90). Your cats might not be too thrilled about this new hobby of yours, but they'll probably stop scratching up the furniture once they realize what could happen to them if they don't behave.

PIG IMPROVEMENT COMPANY, INC.

I f you're into pork, you should definitely acquaint yourself with the Pig Improvement Company, a Kentucky-based multinational devoted to making the world's pigs leaner, healthier, more prolific, and more disease-resistant.

PIC (a maddeningly unsatisfying acronym — why couldn't they have called themselves the Pig Improvement *Group*?), which describes itself as "the largest and most widespread pig breeding company in the world," takes the notion of "pig improvement" quite literally. The firm is essentially a massive eugenics operation, with 10 Ph.D. geneticists on staff. Working in the high-tech PIC labs, employing such techniques as artificial insemination, electronic recording of feed intake, ultrasound, and DNA testing, they isolate this or that gene, eliminate undesirable traits, and generally play Pig God. The ultimate goal is to provide hog farmers with the most productive — and hence profitable — pigs that science can engineer. As one PIC brochure puts it, "30 pigs per sow per year? Not yet, but we're working on it."

PIC's research and development has resulted in the creation of over two dozen genetically pure lines, each one individually tailored to meet the needs of a specific pork market and/or farming community. The PIC 405 boar, for example, is described as an "aggressive" breed of "excellent workers." The 326 boar, on the other hand, is "a synthetic line . . . that produces consistently high yields, a high percentage of lean, and significantly lower levels of backfat." In a shameless attempt to maximize sales, PIC suggests that optimum results can be achieved with the 326 if it is mated with PIC's Camborough 15 gilt, which features "consistently high prolificacy, exceptional mothering, docile temperament, versatility, and a long working life." A photograph depicting a huge litter of piglets frantically scrambling for a nip of a Camborough 15's milk leads one to wonder if the breed's prolificacy may have outstripped its mothering capacity.

All of this information comes from PIC's extensive promotional literature, which features unusually high production values and reads pretty much like a vegetarian's nightmare. The various brochures and presentation sheets are full of bouncy little buzz terms that I imagine are all the rage in the pork biz: "excellent feed conversion," "improved carcass quality," "sow management," "lean performance of terminal boar lines."

Meanwhile, some of the genetics-related material is sufficiently matter-of-fact to be disturbing, even to a devoted carnivore like myself. The following passage, which sounds like what might have been written if Hitler and Shockley had gone into the livestock business together, is typical: "To maximize the rate of genetic change, the boars in the genetic nucleus herds are used for only 25 services and sows average only two litters. They are then replaced by their genetically superior progeny." Call me nostalgic, but this really gets me pining for the days when the swine industry was content to promote itself with catchy slogans like "Pork: The Other White Meat."

MICHAEL INDUSTRIES, INC.

 here's inconspicuous consumption, and then there's inconspicuous production. I was recently given a lesson in the latter by Michael Industries, an Ohio firm that would rather not discuss the product they manufacture and distribute. Bit of a shame, too, because the product in question happens to be a very interesting one: barbed wire.

My interest in Michael Industries began when I spotted one of their ads in a copy of *American Jails* magazine. "Questions About Perimeter Security?" the copy began. "As the number one supplier of barbed wire to the U.S. military, we *know* how to control perimeter areas. . . . We will help you determine the best system for your needs. When barbed wire is part of it, we'll assist you with proper specifications, configuration, and material requirements." Yowza — and to think that I'd been neglecting my perimeter security all this time.

I soon realized that barbed wire is classically inconspicuous. Just take a stroll down any block with a parking lot, a vacant plot of land, or a construction site — the nasty-looking wire is all over the place. But since most of us have no intention of scaling a fence in the first place, we're largely oblivious to the stuff.

As for me, my thoughts about barbed wire pretty much began and ended with several fence-hopping experiences during my occasional forays breaking into abandoned midwestern factories (see Chapter 5). But I started becoming intrigued with the possibilities — a few yards of barbed wire around my record collection, for example, sounded like just the thing to keep the ever-present borrowing brigade at bay. A similar amount of wire might finally convince people to take me seriously when I ask them not to touch some of my more fragile antiques. And a loop or two of razor wire would surely be sufficient to keep the cats away from the dresser drawers they're always scratching up.

With these and other ideas playing through my mind, I was eager to speak to the folks at Michael Industries. But they, as it turned out, were not nearly so eager to speak with me. When repeated phone calls finally got me through to someone named Jim Jones, he essentially erected a barbed-wire fence around himself.

"You want to write about *what?*" he asked.

"Well," I explained for the third time, "I like to examine specialized products and services, and you guys seem pretty damn specialized. So, ideally, I'd like as much information as you're willing to provide about the barbed-wire market, where your company fits into the overall barbed-wire picture, that sort of thing. Oh, and a few samples would be good, too."

"You want *WHAT*?"

Clearly, what Jim and I were experiencing was a failure to communicate. He chose to resolve it in the classic techno-cultural manner — by resorting to a machine. "Look," he said, "just send me a fax explaining what you want."

I did just that, and a week later received a faxed reply from company president Edward P. Murphy: "Thank you for your interest in Michael Industries, Inc. Since we feel our products are of interest to a very limited sector, we prefer that you not pursue an article on our company or its products." Well, as you can see, it's a little late for that now. Which just goes to show that there are some forms of perimeter security that even barbed wire can't reinforce.

FRIGID FLUID COMPANY

T he self-described "deathcare" business, as they say, is pretty much recession-proof. Death, after all, is a fact of life. In fat times or lean, you don't need the actuarial tables to know that loads of people are going to be kicking off, keeling over, buying the farm, rendezvousing with the Grim Reaper, snuffing it — in short, lots of our fellow citizens will be *dying* — and that someone's going to have to handle the burial, the cremation, the funeral, and what have you.

Which is where firms like the Frigid Fluid Company come in. Frigid Fluid, a Chicago outfit specializing in embalming fluids, was brought to my attention by my pal Bettina, who learned of them while rooming with an aspiring mortuary cosmetician (yes, someone who applies make-up to the corpse before a funeral). According to Bettina's roomie, who'd visited the company's offices, the Frigid folks even had a bumper sticker that read, "Get Rigid with Frigid!" So during my next trip to Chicago, a field trip to Frigid HQ was definitely on the agenda.

With Bettina navigating and my friends Tim and Elena along for the ride, we **Typical Frigid Fluid products.** drove over to Frigid's digs, located along a pleasingly industrial stretch on Chicago's West Side. The building itself was unremarkable: a simple office with what looked to be a smallish manufacturing and/or shipping operation out back. None of it looked particularly inviting, and I had a feeling that factory tours were not part of Frigid's community-outreach program.

One very tense encounter with a receptionist later, we were flipping through a copy of Frigid's catalog, a 96-page curiosity that proves death is still alive and kicking. The first several pages are devoted to embalming fluids, including X-20 Arterial Fluid ("Produces desired firming action and a natural, life-like base for cosmetic application"), 36 Plus ("Incorporates new penetrants for abundant drainage"), Flo-Tone ("Completely different! . . . Try it with your most difficult cases!"), Frigid Special ("Should be kept on hand at all times for frozen or refrigerated bodies"), Cavity King ("The Undefeated Fluid of a Hundred Uses. . . . For cases where circulation is destroyed, bodies posted, mutilated, diseased, crushed, dismembered"), Eotone ("Highly recommended for cases that will require cross-country shipment"), 5-Purpose Cavity ("A powerful deodorant against putrefaction, gangrene, and other body odors"), Solvol ("Recommended for embalming infants"), Natural Tone ("Produces 'Living Skin' qualities"), Stop Fluid ("Destroys maggots, lice, and vermin"), and the intriguingly named Premium Jaundice (don't ask).

But fluids, as it turns out, are only a small part of Frigid's distribution business. The rest of the catalog, one section of which is playfully entitled "Sundries," is a mother lode of funeral and cemetery supplies, including such specialized products as face formers, jugular drain tubes, caskets, urns, "Reserved for Funeral" road cones, mortuary cots, funeral home registers, burial suits and undergarments, and a *lot* more. The most entertaining bit is on page 71, which features four wall-mounted crucifixes, one of them stamped, "DISCONTINUED," a reference that presumably applies to the specific ornament shown, not to Christianity itself.

Unfortunately, no prices are listed. When I requested a price sheet from the receptionist, she said, "You don't need a price list; you're not going to be buying anything." And with that she whooshed us out the door, before I could even ask for one of those "Get Rigid with Frigid!" bumper stickers.

LONG ISLAND PRODUCTIONS, INC.

 veryone loves movies, at least in theory. But with Hollywood pumping out an endless stream of boring garbage and the art circuit clogged with pretentious crap, what's a cinemaphile to do? I have three words for you: *industrial safety trailers.*

Long Island Productions is the place to go for short films on such subject areas as construction safety, fire prevention, solid waste disposal, forklift protocol, and proper lifting. The firm's catalog features hundreds of videos, with titles like *Bloodborne Pathogens: The OSHA Standard; Housekeeping and Accident Prevention; Chain Saw Safety; Grinder and Abrasive Wheel Safety; Emergency Elevator Evacuation Procedures; Dog Bite Prevention;* and *Backhoe Safety and Operations.* Most of these run between 10 and 20 minutes and sell for $99; a selection of five-minute vids is also offered, at $49 per. While the prices are steep, the company offers a free 10-day preview of all its wares, providing the perfect opportunity to order a few dozen titles, throw an industrial-video party for yourself and all your friends, and then send everything back with no charge and no obligation.

BORDEN CONSUMER RESPONSE DEPARTMENT

 f course, in the final analysis, the only true service is *customer* service. In the case of the letter reproduced on the next page, I trust it's self-explanatory.

BORDEN, INC.

CONSUMER RESPONSE DEPARTMENT
BORDEN, INC.
180 EAST BROAD ST., COLUMBUS, OHIO 43215

IF IT'S BORDEN, IT'S
GOT TO BE GOOD

August 11, 1988

Mr. Paul Lukas
209 Wyckoff Street
Brooklyn NY 11217

Dear Mr. Lukas:

Thank you for your letter regarding Cracker Jack.

We were sorry to learn that your recent box did not contain a prize. This is
contrary to a tradition started in 1912 when toy surprises were first
introduced in the product.

The anticipation of a toy surprise is part of the enjoyment almost everyone
expects from Cracker Jack. Even today, kids of all ages can hardly wait to
open the box to see what's inside.

Our Cracker Jack packages are filled by high speed equipment with peanuts and
prizes added automatically. There are three electronic eyes on every
production line to help assure a prize is packed in every container. However,
even the best of people and machines cannot be 100% accurate, and occasionally
a box may leave the factory without a toy surprise.

Please accept our apologies for the disappointment this situation has caused.
Enclosed is a complimentary coupon, as well as a few toy surprises we hope you
will enjoy.

Sincerely,

Consumer Representative
Consumer Response Dept.

SEVEN

Talk about inconspicuous — in a society whose idea of literature has become the back of a baseball card, the printed word is the biggest extinct dinosaur of them all. Throw in the Internet and it becomes apparent that the long-held supremacy of printed matter is due to be supplanted any moment. Still, for those who find a quaint sort of pleasure in this sort of thing (you *are* reading this book, after all), the following items offer instructive lessons in the enduring utility of ink on paper.

THE PENTAGRAM PAPERS

F or several years I paid the rent by editing books written by graphic designers. One of the niftier aspects of this arrangement — aside from dealing with generally interesting, intelligent authors and working with some really fun artwork — was that I managed to get myself added to very rewarding mailing lists. Paper companies, for instance, send out heaps of engaging samples, all beautifully packaged and produced, to anyone even vaguely connected with the design world. And design firms often send imaginative toys as self-promotional pieces. Once you get on a mailing list for such trinkets you can stay there for a long time, even if, like myself, you've moved on to other areas of work.

Of all the design-related freebies I've received, the ones I've come to value most are the Pentagram Papers, a series of small, lovingly produced pamphlets and books created by Pentagram, a fancy-shmancy design partnership. Distributed now and again as a sort of serial demonstration of Pentagram's wit and cleverness (a standard self-promotional approach in the design world), the Pentagram Papers offer nugget after nugget of truly endearing visual ephemera in bite-sized form. One edition features starkly beautiful extreme-close-up photos of a variety of writing implements (pen, quill, charcoal, chalk, etc.); another gives simple, beautifully illustrated instructions on how to draw anything from an equilateral triangle to a perfect nonagon using nothing more than a compass and a ruler; another offers a well-executed take on the snappy-comebacks routine, appealingly entitled *A Child's Treasury of Smart-Ass Remarks.* As you might expect, design and production values are very high throughout.

PENTAGRAM

The Pentagram Papers, unfortunately, are not for sale or otherwise available to mere mortals outside the rather insular confines of what I like to call the Design Mafia, and I'm not sure how you can get on the list for them. But don't let that stop you — call or write to Pentagram, claim to be a potential client, and maybe they'll send you some.

DOUBLE RED'S LUCKY NUMBER VISIONS · · · · · · · · · · · · · ·
VAL'S ORIGINAL GENUINE BIG GREEN DAILY &
WEEKLY LOTTERY SHEET

Several years ago I had a really bad day at work. I mean a *really* bad day — the kind of day that makes you want to go in and waste your boss with an M-16, regardless of the consequences. The kind of day, in short, that makes playing the lottery suddenly look like an attractive alternative. Although this desperate "need" to win a big pot of gold eventually subsided (I switched jobs), I continued to play Lotto almost every week for the next few years, at one point winning $100, until my enthusiasm for the game waned. I might not have stopped playing, however, had I been aware of the numerous lottery tipsheets available at newsstands throughout New York City.

A typical example is *Double Red's Lucky Number Visions,* a monthly 16-page pamphlet with a nice two-color cover, making it rather upscale for this type of publication. Retailing for $1.25, *Double Red's* features lots of numerical tables and charts, special birthday betting tips, and plenty of astrology-based advice. Leos, for example, are counseled thusly: "Changing your bets too soon will short-change your game. Give your bets time to mature by playing each selection for at least ten days."

Double Red himself, who appears here and there throughout the book, is depicted as a swashbuckling, mustachioed mystery man — kind of like the Kissing Bandit. He's the sort of

Double Red Says

Double Red Numerologist

Traveling Triples 000 999

166
611

881
118

979
797

When you play a double, Always play the mirror number. *
*Sometimes called the "cousin".

002
200

335 553

929

DOUBLE RED PUBLISHING

benevolent numerologist who no doubt helps old ladies across the street when he isn't authoring the "Number Advice" column that runs on the pamphlet's inside back cover. Here he offers such helpful betting suggestions as "There are no hard and fast rules. You've got to use your judgment," and "We suggest you pick up some copies of our other publications."

If you somehow strike out with Double Red, you might want to try *Val's Original Genuine Big Green Daily & Weekly Lottery Sheet*, a weekly that'll set you back a buck. It really is just a sheet — an 8.5-by-14-inch sheet, to be exact — xeroxed on both sides and folded up like a train schedule. What I really like about *Val's* is that in spite of this low-tech approach, it has its very own bar code, clearly a beacon of legitimacy amidst a sea of scurrilous publications looking to rip you off.

Val's features a profusion of tables, including the rather ingenious "Long Overdue" table, which lists the numbers that are, well, long overdue to be chosen in the various daily numbers games. *Val's* also functions nicely as a reference guide, providing breakdowns of every number chosen

VAL PUBLISHING Co.

in the area's games over the past year. Given its simple format, *Val's* is really stuffed to the gills with useful info. Indeed, as a note from the publisher obligingly points out, "There are thousands of numbers and lottery players all over the country who aren't as fortunate as you because this numbers and lottery sheet is not on sale in their area." The thought of so many benighted souls brings a tear to the eye. I ask you, is this an unfair world or what?

UNITED STATES ARMY TECHNICAL AND FIELD MANUALS

F or years the standard source for bizarro how-to literature has been the Loompanics catalog. But why put up with lousy desktop-publishing graphics, spotty writing, and someone else's profit margin when you can be entertained just as well by your own tax dollars at work? Your friend and mine, the United States Army, has published an informative series of books that tell you how to survive in hostile environments, how to manufacture and use explosives, and how to kill the other guy before he kills you. Available at any decent Army-Navy store for about eight bucks a pop, these manuals represent Washington's *real* idea of a civics lesson, and the collapse of the Cold War hasn't led any of them to go out of print.

A typical example is the *Boobytraps* field manual, first published in 1965, a handy little volume that explores surreptitious explosives in all their varied glory. Special sections are devoted to basic boobytrapping doctrine, boobytrapping buildings, disarming methods, and my favorite, "Improvisations." Nicely rendered illustrations show how to rig a canteen, pen, flashlight, or whiskey bottle for detonation. This all sounds like loads more fun than either a

Figure 185. Improvised sunglasses.

From the *Survival* field manual.

whoopee cushion or a lamp shade on your head, and no special knowledge of chemistry or electronics is needed for any of it—just follow the instructions and you'll be the hit of your next dinner party.

Almost as good is the *Incendiaries* tech manual (1966), part of the "Unconventional Warfare Devices and Techniques" series. Straightforwardly written and genuinely educational, this edition features chapters on initiators, igniters, delay mechanisms, and every pyromaniac's dream, spontaneous combustion. And if you're worried about the subject matter being a bit dry, forget about it— as the text makes abundantly clear, there's no reason we can't maintain a sense of humor while plotting how to blow up a row of houses. One of the more effective igniters, for instance, is a sugar/potassium-chlorate mixture

Figure 34. Using a stick to crack a coconut.

jocularly known as "fire fudge."

The best book of the lot is the *Survival* field manual (1970), 285 pages of sage advice like "Never eat polar bear meat unless it is properly cooked. It

ROCK WEIGHT — PARACHUTE BUCKLE
BAIT
STOCKADE

Figure 130. A fall log trap for big game.

U.S. DEPARTMENT OF DEFENSE

is always diseased" and "Don't fool around [with] native women. . . . When women are given liberty there is almost a venereal disease certainty," along with lots of talk about how to "control your sweating." Helpful diagrams show just how easy it is to crack a coconut, capture big game, construct a tepee, make your own improvised sunglasses (fashionable!), design a roasting and steaming pit, or even divert a stream. And while you probably already knew that grubs and other bugs can be eaten for their protein value, were you also aware that they make excellent stock for soup? Seen in this informed context, being stranded in the jungle or at the North Pole or in the desert doesn't seem like such a bad deal. Why, the world is your oyster, as long as you cook it properly.

"DEAR DOTTI" ADVICE COLUMN • • • • • • • • • • • • • •

O kay, so by now everyone knows that the *Weekly World News* is cool. But do you know why? Here's a hint: It has nothing to do with space aliens, 89-year-old women giving birth to 75-pound babies, or the Loch Ness Monster.

As far as I'm concerned, the weekly musings of advice columnist Dotti Primrose are worth the price of admission to *WWN*'s freak show. Forget about Ann Landers or Dear Abby—you can bet that if Dotti ever ran into those two simps, she'd kick 'em in the shins, steal their purses, and throw in a facelift joke for good measure. And unlike Ann and Abby, Dotti'll never be found dispensing such worthless scraps of alleged advice as "See a therapist" or "Please get counseling, and write to me soon to let me know how you're doing—I care." Her responses more typically run along the lines of "A lot of people don't have the smarts to get ahead in the world. You're obviously one of them!" and "You sound like a real loser—no wonder you live in a trailer park."

As entertaining as Dotti is, there's no denying that her column was more fun back in the 1980s, when her mug shot depicted her looking bored while reading the latest letter from the oh-so-troubled legions, her face a perfect picture of bemused disgust. The photo they're running these days shows Dotti looking intrigued, as if the letter she's reading might actually be interesting. Fortunately, in spite of this photographic concession to civility, advice like "Why don't you give her a voodoo doll—with a hat pin stuck right through the head?" keeps me coming back for more. The fact that the entire column—letters *and* responses—is probably written by a bunch of underpaid journalism school dropouts doesn't bother me one bit.

WEEKLY
WORLD NEWS,
INC.

THE 1991 INFORMATION PLEASE ALMANAC

We all know there is only one real criterion when assessing a book's true value: Does it make for good bathroom reading? Record and film guides are good, but if you're like me you've already memorized them all. Anything baseball-related is fine, but then you've got the problem of seasonality.

For sheer trivia overload and addictive page-turning, nothing beats a good almanac. As you can see, mine is a few years out of date, but that's okay—there's really no need to buy more than one per decade. Open to any page you like, you can't go wrong. Look, here's a half-page synopsis of the

Civil War; here's a year-by-year listing of major headlines in history; here's a breakdown of "Volcanoes of the World"; here's a chart detailing the typical gestation periods and life spans for various animals; here's a crash course on the planets in our solar system; here's a glossary of weather-related terms; here's a table of famous firsts in aviation; here's a quick summary of postal regulations.

HOUGHTON MIFFLIN COMPANY

I could go on, but I think you get the idea. More than 1,000 pages, and you'll still get change from a ten-spot. Just try to remember that someone's waiting to get into the can after you, okay?

"BAZOOKA JOE & COMPANY" COMIC STRIP

Remember Bazooka Joe? He was a runty little guy, kinda looked like Popeye Jr. with an eye patch, only for some reason he was the coolest guy on his block.

I hadn't seen him since I was a kid, so I went down to the local candy store to get reacquainted. I found that the Bazooka Joe I knew is long gone, and I hold his bubble-gum company responsible.

For openers, it used to be "Bazooka Joe and His *Gang*" (emphasis mine), but I guess that was deemed too provocative a title for a world filled with restless urban youth, so now it's "& Company." How limp. Moreover, Joe and his colleagues have been totally retooled for the MTV era: slick hairstyles, chic sunglasses, acid-washed jeans jackets, off-the-shoulder dresses for the girls, and so on. The nadir can be found in "Bazooka Joe Raps," an assortment of predictably awful rhymin'-and-stylin' strips that make up about

20 percent of the current series and find Joe resorting to self-referential salesmanship ("So read my strip, have some fun/And pass the time as you chew my gum!"), something the old Bazooka Joe *never* would've done.

Want more bad news? As you may recall, it was once possible to redeem a few dozen of Joe's comics plus some small change for such essential cheapo merchandise as military-style dog tags, ball/strike counters, plastic-bodied mini-cameras ("Really works!"), and decoder-style rings. Well today, my friend, 100 Bazooka Joe comics plus a token will get you a ride on the subway, dig? Plus the gum now costs a nickel and tastes like cotton candy rolled in septic waste. I say boycott the stuff.

The Topps Company, Inc.

AMERICAN CEMETERY MAGAZINE
AMERICAN FUNERAL DIRECTOR MAGAZINE

These fine trade publications serve as useful reminders that behind every industry — the deathcare industry, in this case — there's a slew of internal politics, petty self-importance, and entertaining merchandise lines.

As the Frigid Fluid Company's catalog clearly demonstrates (see Chapter 6), the death biz offers some extremely interesting products. It therefore comes as no surprise that the best things in these magazines are the ads — even a small percentage of the items advertised herein would keep me fascinated for months: hydraulic lifts designed to hoist caskets into mausoleums; heaters that quickly thaw out frozen ground (for when you need to dig that midwinter grave, silly); an amazingly wide-ranging selection of designer urns;

a face mask to keep your friendly neighborhood embalming staff safe from any stray fluids that might spurt out of someone's disease-ridden corpse; an assortment of industrial-strength cremators and mortuary refrigerators. They've got solutions to problems you don't even want to *know* about.

But hey, the editorial features are cool, too: the latest installment of the monthly "Funerals of the Famous" feature ("Millard Fillmore: A Grand Send-Off for an Unheralded President"); a nice essay on improving community relations ("Open the gates and show the community what a rich resource the cemetery can be," they urge, while suggesting such crowd-pleasing activities as grave-rubbings and, I swear, *scavenger hunts*—the mind fairly boggles); industry-specific craftsmanship features ("Casketmakers Create Memorable Pieces of Art"); and simple news tidbits ("Death Rate Up a Bit in First Quarter"). Best of all may be the extensive coverage of the annual National Association of Funeral Directors convention, where the keynote speakers have included such luminaries as John Sununu, who was paid $15,000 for his efforts and looks like he got a free embalming in the bargain.

IN PERSON, IN TIME MANUAL

T he life-threatening aspects of police work may seem like the toughest part of the job, but take a moment to consider the pressures associated with notifying the next of kin in the event of a death. Dodging bullets and dealing with drug-crazed, knife-wielding thugs probably aren't any fun, but death notification is a uniquely stressful experience. So there must be a day or two devoted to the subject during police academy training, right?

Well, maybe everyone was cutting class that day, because it turns out that death notification is among the things that cops tend not to handle too well. For starters, they're often inexcusably slow to reach the next of kin, which leaves families to learn the bad news through the media, frequently in traumatic fashion. And when the police finally get around to it, they're often remarkably careless with their language, making offhand comments that just compound a bad situation.

I learned all of this from *In Person, In Time: Recommended Procedures for Death Notification,* a report recently published by the Iowa State Attorney General's office. The guidelines set forth here are simple and sensible: "Notification should be done in person, in time, in pairs whenever possible, in plain language, and with compassion."

It's the bit about using "plain language" that appears to be the biggest stickler. According to the report, policemen have a disturbing tendency to refer to the deceased as "the body," and they've also been known to make such brilliant statements as, "She led a full life," and, "It was God's will." *In Person, In Time* recommends that officers begin by saying, "I have some very bad news to tell you," and counsels them to avoid vague descriptions like, "Sally was lost" or "John passed away." Instead, says the manual, just be direct: "Your daughter was in a car crash and she was killed," or, "Your father had a heart attack at his workplace and he died."

Despite clocking in at only 18 pages, the report is quite thorough, covering a variety of death-notification situations, including notification in the workplace or at a hospital. An assortment of forms and resource listings are provided for distribution to survivors, and there's even a set of 20 wallet-

IOWA STATE DEPARTMENT OF JUSTICE

sized cards for officers to use, each listing the essential points covered in the report, much like the classic Miranda warning cards. While all of this would appear to run counter to the old "Grandma was playing on the roof . . ." joke, *In Person, In Time* is a laudable — and apparently long overdue — response to a sensitive situation.

EROTIC SEXUAL POSITIONS FROM AROUND THE WORLD BOOKLET

W ith AIDS and unwanted pregnancy being what they are, you'd think most restroom condom machines would be stocked with, you know, condoms. But the more bars I visit, the more I find these vending apparatuses loaded with the sort of novelty items that I thought had vacated the market along with stag films. Let's face it, you'd have to be pretty damn drunk to find even 50 cents' worth of entertainment value in a Space Panties Gift Certificate or a Quickie-Nookie Instant Marriage License.

Erotic Sexual Positions from Around the World, however, a 32-page booklet that my friend Christine scored in the women's room of the enjoyable if overlit Troy's Lounge in Rodeo, California, is like the nibble on the end of your line that keeps you fishing all day. I'll gladly wade through piles of novelty midget rubbers and garishly decorated French ticklers if I can land even one more condom-machine product this entertaining.

With its 1.75-by-1.25-inch oblong trim size and lean page count, *Erotic Sexual Positions* would make a swell Cracker Jack toy. Each of the booklet's 16 spreads features a page of text on a given sexual position or technique, accompanied by a line illustration of a Ken-and-Barbie-ish couple engaged in said activity. The publisher's stated goal is "helping you become a worldly lover," and they mean that in the most literal sense—each highlighted sexual specialty hails from a different area of the globe. Hence we get to learn about such, uh, exotic practices as French kissing (an "import from romantic France"), 69 ("a popular substitute for intercourse in Latin countries"), and what the text officially terms "Doggie Rear Entry Position" ("Eighteenth-century England is responsible for this famous position"). My favorite is the spread devoted to standing cunnilingus, attributed to "Arctic men [who] instituted this diversion for a hot night in a cold climate." Maybe I'm just being picky, but I somehow doubt that the Arctic men's wives and girlfriends were wearing high heels like those shown on the babe in the accompanying illustration.

Unlike most condom-machine novelties, *Erotic Sexual Positions* takes more than 10 seconds to read and assess (more like five to 10 very amusing minutes, which isn't bad at all for 50 cents), and I can vouch from personal experience that it brings a barroom pool game to a dead stop. Best of all, the back cover promises that this booklet is just the "first of a series of Erotic Best Sellers." Cool—where do I subscribe?

SIGHTINGS POSTCARD SERIES

ots of art projects make use of found objects, but few do so as simply and cleverly as *Sightings*, a series of postcards based on snapshots found around New York City and Canada. The images serve up a steady diet of routine mundanity that should strike a familiar chord among those who collect found photos (or can honestly assess their own photo albums): a preppy-ish guy dancing at a party, a smiling man and his granddaughter relaxing on a lounge chair in the backyard, a tacky-looking girl posing near the water at a marina—you get the idea. In keeping with the spirit of found art, no attempt has been made to clean up the images; if part of the original photo was scratched or grainy or underexposed, then the postcard is, too.

Things get more interesting when you turn the cards over. The upper-left region of the back of a postcard, of course, is traditionally reserved for a caption describing the image on the front, and the *Sightings* cards rigidly adhere to this protocol while exhibiting an impressive attention to detail. A typical caption in the series reads, "One of six photographs found in trash can, November 1992, 8th Avenue at 20th Street, New York, verso stamped in pink ink, 'APRIL 1992.'" Another: "Photograph found 17 May 1993, 41st Street at Dyer Avenue, New York, verso imprinted, '11 + 00 NNNN 818 + 02'; marked, 'FUJICOLOR paper'; and inscribed in black ink, 'Christmas 1991 / (seated) Peter, Elizabeth, Rosie / (foreground) Claire.'"

Sightings is the work of Germaine Koh, a Canadian conceptual artist who started collecting found photos in 1991 and began turning them into postcards in 1993. Her promotional literature, which she uses to pitch the project to galleries, describes the postcards as "operating in the anonymous realm between lost and found, as enigmatic markers of the passage of specific unknown people through time and space. . . . They engage our allegiances to private objects and communal spaces, singular fetishes and common types [and] deal with both theoretical and physical consequences of property and representation." Koh concedes that much of this language is a bit "overblown" but finds it necessary to resort to such verbiage in the highly competitive art world. *Sightings* sounds much more interesting when she tells me, "One important thing that I underplay in the project description is that it's just a really cool idea." She's right.

THE WILD PARTY, BY JOSEPH MONCURE MARCH, WITH ILLUSTRATIONS BY ART SPIEGELMAN

Maybe you can't judge a book by its cover, but that isn't a bad place to start. Conventional schools of thought may consider books important for their literary value, but I'm frankly more interested in them as objects. Whether you realize it or not, you probably agree with me, as evidenced by the hundreds of books that no doubt clutter up your home. I've always been puzzled by this tendency — books, unlike records, can't be pulled off the shelf and enjoyed in their entirety in 45 minutes, and I'd bet right now that it's been years since you reread or even consulted any of the nonreference titles in your collection. The more book-obsessed you are, in fact, the more likely you are to be acquiring a steady stream of new books, leaving you no time to go back to the old ones. So what are you saving them for? The answer, I submit, is simple: for material satisfaction.

With this standard in mind, let's examine *The Wild Party* on the basis of its material and physical characteristics alone. More specifically, let's examine its *endpapers*.

Every hardcover book has endpapers, but you probably don't think about them very much. Endpapers are those sheets at the beginning and end of the book — they're glued to the inside front and back covers and also to the printed signatures, which means they literally hold the book together. But they're usually just plain white paper and look like blank pages, which is why nobody pays much attention to them.

PANTHEON BOOKS

Projects with hefty production budgets, like art books, sometimes have colored endpapers, an indulgence that costs a few pennies more per unit but adds tremendous objective appeal. Fancier books up the ante even higher by printing art, text, or maps on the endpapers.

But this book—a reissue of a "lost classic," or hucksterish words to that effect—is the first volume I've ever encountered that features *felt endpapers,* a stroke of manufacturing genius that takes this once humble production element into decadent strata previously undreamed of by reader or bookbinder. The red felt is so pleasant to the touch that I've permanently removed the dust jacket from my copy of the book, just so my left index finger can have unimpeded access to stroke the felt-lined inside front cover as I read. You can go ahead and have your information stuporhighway —my index finger and I know what *real* interactive literary pleasure is all about, and you'll never find felt endpapers on the Internet.

THE IRAN-CONTRA SCANDAL: THE DECLASSIFIED HISTORY, EDITED BY PETER KORNBLUH AND MALCOLM BYRNE

Most books are content just to be books. But for a volume such as this one—a big, hardbound presentation of heretofore classified government documents, published by a high-minded press—being a mere book is not enough. In this case, it is necessary to be a *tome.*

Tomehood is primarily a function of heft, an element that we might further define as size times weight. A true tome should be too big to fit in your day bag and sufficiently substantial to double as a medicine ball. *The Iran-Contra Scandal* scores well on the first part of this equation, clocking in at 448 pages, with a healthy $7\frac{7}{8}$-by-10-inch trim size and a most impressive $1\frac{1}{4}$-inch bulk. Pick the book up, however, and it's amazingly light for its size—two pounds nine ounces, to be exact. If you tried to swat a fly with this book, the fly would probably win.

The key is in the paper, a rather grainy 55-pound stock called Perfection Antique that bulks up deceptively well, undoubtedly chosen by the publisher to create the *illusion* of tomehood (perhaps to justify the tomelike $40 retail price). By way of comparison, I pulled a few books of similar trim size off my shelf and found that Richard Penner's *Conference Center Planning and Design* (Whitney, 1990) and Lynn Pecktal's *Costume Design* (Back Stage, 1993) both run 192 pages shorter than *The Iran-Contra Scandal* but weigh in at an ounce *heavier*. The nitpickers among you might point out that these two examples are both printed on glossy-coated stock, which tends to be inherently heavy, but I'm compelled to point out that George C. Kohn's *Encyclopedia of American Scandal* (Facts on File, 1989), which runs 48 pages shorter than *Iran-Contra* and is printed on no-frills, uncoated paper, tips the scales at 2 pounds 14 ounces—five ounces heavier. There's no getting around it: *The Iran-Contra Scandal* may look impressively imposing, but it's really just a welterweight wearing a heavyweight's trunks. Our nation's shelving systems need not tremble in fear of its arrival.

THE
NEW PRESS

INCONSPICUOUS STATISTICS

Consumer culture is a complex and esoteric exercise that generally defies numerical applications. That's why large corporations employ such hefty marketing and advertising staffs — if consumerism could all be reduced to a mathematical formula, it would be much simpler (if less interesting) for everyone involved. Still, for those who insist that nothing is real or substantial until its numbers have been duly crunched, here are some facts and figures about the two years it took to write this book:

Number of subjects formally reviewed: 105

Approximate ratio of subjects seriously considered for review to those actually making the cut: 8 to 1

Number of abandoned industrial sites broken into in an attempt to find interesting artifacts: 4

Number of friends who coincidentally mentioned kraut juice to me over a 17-day period: 3

Number of foodstuffs consumed that I never would have tried otherwise: 11*

Number of good-tasting foodstuffs consumed that I never would have tried otherwise: 2

Number of foodstuffs encountered that I couldn't and/or wouldn't consume: 2*

Number of pet products consumed with a "How bad could it be?" attitude: 1

*Figure listed refers only to the 105 products reviewed in the book; actual total compiled in the course of researching the book is significantly higher.

Number of customer-service departments contacted for additional information: 12*

Number of corporate marketing departments contacted for additional information: 21*

Approximate percentage of these combined encounters that might be characterized as "pleasant": 75

Number of companies that refused to speak with me: 2*

Number of times put on hold by a Hershey's consumer-response representative during a single phone call, each time being forced to listen to opera: 4

Number of irate letters received from outraged kraut juice partisans after I wrote about the product in my 'zine: 1

Number of very nice conversations with presidents of National Football League franchises about their teams' uniform designs: 1

Number of shoe stores visited in an attempt to order my very own Brannock Device: 3

Number of miles' worth of string used each year to make the string handles on Animal Crackers boxes, according to a Nabisco fact sheet: 6,000

Number of Toast-O-Lators seen at flea markets selling for about six times what I paid for mine: 2

Number of cats in my household who've gone bonkers over Real-Fur Mouse cat toys: 3

Approximate number of Real-Fur Mice ripped to shreds by said cats from 1987 through 1995: 75

ADDRESSES

E very attempt has been made to verify the addresses of the firms and organizations whose products and services are discussed in this volume. Still, readers should bear in mind that some companies move, others get gobbled up by larger companies, still others simply go out of business, and a few stubbornly resisted my efforts to track them down. That said, most of the ones referred to in the preceding pages can be found at the following addresses, which are listed in the order of their appearance in the text.

CHAPTER ONE

The Brannock Device Company, 116 Luther Ave., Liverpool, NY 13088

American Science & Surplus, 3605 Howard St., Skokie, IL 60076

Jonathan Law, P.O. Box 254, Kennebunkport, ME 04046

The Dial-a-Pick Co., Inc., P.O. Box 12061, San Antonio, TX 78212

G.M. Steakhouse, 626 N. Lamar, Austin, TX 78703

American Traffic Information, Inc., 1897 Clove Rd., Staten Island, NY 10304

CHAPTER TWO

Woodstream Corporation, 69 N. Locust St., Lititz, PA 17543

The United States Postal Service, c/o the Postmaster General, 475 L'Enfant Plaza, Washington, DC 20260

The Wool Bureau, 330 Madison Ave., 19th fl., New York, NY 10017

Alpo Petfoods, Inc., 2050 Pope Road, Allentown, PA 18104

Ohio Art Co., 1 Toy St., Bryan, OH 43506

Johnson & Johnson Consumer Products, Inc., 199 Grandview Rd., Skillman, NJ 08558

Stylex, Inc., 740 Cooper Town Rd., Delanco, NJ 08075

Better Houseware Corp., 25-12 41st Ave., Long Island City, NY 11101

Kimberly-Clark Corporation, P.O. Box 2020, Neenah, WI 54957

The Hoover Company, 101 East Maple St., North Canton, OH 44720

Vo-Toys, Inc., 400 S. 5th St., Harrison, NJ 07029

W. L. Gore & Associates, 1500 N. Fourth St., Flagstaff, AZ 86003

Scott Paper Company, Scott Plaza One, Philadelphia, PA 19113-1510

Binney & Smith Inc., P.O. Box 431, Easton, PA 18044-0431

Green Bay Packers, P.O. Box 10628, Green Bay, WI 54307-0628

Concord Enterprises, Inc., 2957 E. 46th St., Los Angeles, CA 90058

CHAPTER THREE

BeautiControl Cosmetics, Inc., P.O. Box 815189, Dallas, TX 75381

Brice Creations, 112 Conselyea St., Brooklyn, NY 11211

Anatomical Chart Company, 8221 Kimball, Skokie, IL 60076

Schuster's of Texas, Inc., 2109 Priddy Rd., Goldthwaite, TX 76844

The Safety Zone, Hanover, PA 17333-0019

The Weather Channel, 2600 Cumberland Pkwy., Atlanta, GA 30339; for even juicier weather-porn, try the Tornado Video Classics series from the Tornado Project, P.O. Box 302, St. Johnsbury, VT 05819

Monticello Drug Company, 1604 Stockton St., Jacksonville, FL 32204

Project "Young One," Inc., 2125 West Lawn Ave., Racine, WI 53405

Innovative Marketing Alliance, 34184-B Pacific Coast Highway, Suite 312, Dana Point, CA 92629

The Original Pet Drink Co., Inc., 1 E. Broward Blvd., Suite 1505, Fort Lauderdale, FL 33301

LA-CO Industries, Inc., 250 Washtenaw Ave., Chicago, IL 60612

CHAPTER FOUR

Nabisco Brands, Inc./Nabisco Foods, Inc., 200 Deforest Ave., East Hanover, NJ 07936

Reser's Finer Foods, 15570 Southwest Jenkins Rd., Beaverton, OR 97006

Bedessee Imports Inc., 140 Varick Ave., Brooklyn, NY 11237

Rob Salamida Co., 133 Washington Ave., Endicott, NY 13760

SS Lollipop, 179 Pomeroy, Pismo Beach, CA 93449

Continental Baking Company, Checkerboard Square, St. Louis, MO 63164

Bar Food Products, 1052 W. Fulton, Chicago, IL 60607

Snyder's Tavern, Route 28A, W. Shokan, NY 12494

Stokely USA, Inc., 1055 Corporate Center Dr., Oconomowoc, WI 53066

The Fremont Company, Box 845, Fremont, OH 43420

Comstock Foods, 90 Linden Oaks, Rochester, NY 14625

S&W Fine Foods, Inc., 3160 Crow Canyon Rd., San Ramon, CA 94583

National Kraut Packers Association, P.O. Box 606, St. Charles, IL 60174

Curtice Burns Meat Snacks, Inc., 208 S. Kalamath, Denver, CO 80223

Reuther's Seafood Company, Inc., 600 Mazant St., New Orleans, LA 70150

Procter & Gamble, Box 5560, Cincinnati, OH 45202

Home Care Industries, Inc., 1 Lisbon St., Clifton, NJ 07013

Goya Foods, Inc., 100 Seaview Dr., Secaucus, NJ 07094

American Home Food Products, Inc., 5 Giralda Farms, Madison, NJ 07940

Nestlé Confectioners Ltd., Level 11, 12 Help St., Chatswood NSW 2067, Australia

Natural Choices, Inc., 2300 Candelaria Rd. NE, Albuquerque, NM 87107

Otsuka Pharmaceuticals' address is printed in Japanese; their phone number, however, is 011-81-3-3292-0021

Angostura International Ltd., 20 Commerce Dr., Cranford, NJ 07016

Sunshine Biscuits, Inc., 100 Woodbridge Center Dr., Woodbridge, NJ 07095-1196

General Mills, Inc., 1 General Mills Blvd., Minneapolis, MN 55440

Nature's Best, Hauppauge, 195 Engineer's Rd., NY 11788

Sathers Inc., Sather Plaza, Round Lake, MN 56167

Coors Brewing Company, P.O. Box 4030, Golden, CO 80401

Amurol Confections, 2800 N. Rt. 47, Yorkville, IL 60560

CHAPTER FIVE

Brunswick Bowling & Billiards Corporation, 525 West Laketon Ave., Mukegon, MI 49443

J. M. Galef Co., 1414 Ave. of the Americas, New York, NY 10019

CHAPTER SIX

The Society for Industrial Archeology, Dept. of Social Sciences, Michigan Technological University, 1400 Townsend Dr., Houghton, MI 49931

National Park Service, Dept. of the Interior Building, 1849 C St. NW, Washington, DC 20240

Grand Canyon National Park, Box 129, Grand Canyon, AZ 86023

Ferrell Reed, 5571 Arapahoe Ave., Boulder, CO 80303

Cold Trail Mail Co., P.O. Box 874211, Wasilla, AK 99687

Invention Submission Corporation, 217 9th St., Pittsburgh, PA 15222

The American Watch Co., 2846 Misty Morning Rd., Torrance, CA 90505

Firefox Enterprises Inc., P.O. Box 5366, Pocatello, ID 83202

Philip Morris U.S.A., 120 Park Ave., New York, NY 10017

Van Dyke Supply Company, P.O. Box 278, Woonsocket, SD 57385

Pig Improvement Company, Inc., P.O. Box 348, Franklin, KY 42135

Michael Industries, 23 Sisal St., Newark, OH 43055

Frigid Fluid Company, 465 N. Desplaines St., Chicago, IL 60610

Long Island Productions, 1432 Kearney St., El Cerrito, CA 94530

Borden, Inc., 180 E. Broad St., Columbus, OH 43215

CHAPTER SEVEN

Pentagram, 212 Fifth Ave., New York, NY 10010

Double Red Publishing, P.O. Box 4468, Allentown, PA 18105

Val Publishing Co., P.O. Box 731, Mount Vernon, NY 10551

The U.S. Department of Defense, the Pentagon, Washington, DC 20301

Weekly World News, Inc., 600 South East Coast Ave., Lantana, FL 33462

Houghton Mifflin Company, 2 Park St., Boston, MA 02108

The Topps Company, Inc., York Ave., Duryea, PA 18642

The American Cemetery, Inc., 1501 Broadway, New York, NY 10036

Kates-Boylston Publications, Inc., 1501 Broadway, New York, NY 10036

Iowa State Dept. of Justice, Crime Victim Assistance Division, Old Historical Building, Des Moines, IA 50319

Troy's Lounge, First St., Rodeo, CA 94572

Sightings, c/o Germaine Koh, P.O. Box 20032, Ottawa, Ontario K1N 9N5, Canada

Pantheon, 201 E. 50th St., New York, NY 10022

The New Press, 450 W. 41st St., New York, NY 10036

INDEX

ABOUT THE AUTHOR

Joe Zizzo

Paul Lukas lives in Brooklyn, New York, where he began publishing *Beer Frame: The Journal of Inconspicuous Consumption* in 1993. His "Inconspicuous Consumption" column is a bi-weekly feature in *New York* magazine, and he appears weekly on CNNfn's *Biz Buzz*.

To keep up with inconspicuous consumption, read *Beer Frame: The Journal of Inconspicuous Consumption*. For a sample copy, send $3.00 (cash, check, or money order payable to Paul Lukas) to Beer Frame, 160 St. John's Place, Brooklyn, NY 11217.